SUCCESS AND
SATISFACTION
in Your Office Job

SUCCESS AND SATISFACTION
in Your Office Job

by ESTHER R. BECKER
Author of *Secretaries Who Succeed*
and RICHARD L. LAWRENCE

18710

HARPER & BROTHERS, *Publishers, New York*

Library of Congress catalog card number: 54-6440

Acknowledgments

THE authors acknowledge with thanks permission to make quotations from or references to the following: Air Reduction Company, Inc., New York, as mentioned in *Manpower Budgeting Control*, by James W. Quigg, American Management Association; Altrusa International Club; American Institute of Banking; American Institute of Family Relations, Los Angeles; Sherman Billingsley, Stork Club, N.Y.C.; Bristol-Myers Products Division for "The Girl for the Job"; Margaret A. Brown, Standard Oil Company of Ohio, Cleveland; Burns and Roe, Inc. N.Y.C.; Doris Blake, *New York Daily News; Business Education World; Charm* for "You Are a Stenographer and You Want to Move Up," June, 1953; *Collier's*, for "Emotional Upsets Are Good for You," by Howard Whitman, September 4, 1953; *Cosmopolitan*, for "These Secretaries Make Big Money," by Michael Drury, March, 1951; Beatrice Desfosses, speech consultant, Berkeley Schools, New York, White Plains and East Orange, N.J.; Eaton Paper Corporation, Pittsfield, Mass., for *A Handbook of Office Behavior*, 1950; Helen Edwards and Staff, Los Angeles; Ethyl Corporation, N.Y.C.; *Factory Management and Maintenance*, June, 1953; Katharine Gibbs Schools, as mentioned in "How to Educate a Secretary," *Saturday Evening Post*, February 12, 1949; Dr. Lydia G. Giberson, Personal Adviser, Metropolitan Life Insurance Company; *Glamour*, issues copyrighted January, 1950, December, 1952, and September, 1953; Condé Nast Publications, Inc.; Gregg Publishing Company, for *Practical Business Psychology*, by Donald A. and Eleanor C. Laird, 1951; *Harvard Business Review*, for "Opportunities for Women at the Administrative Level," by Frances M. Fuller and Mary B. Batchelder, January-February, 1953; Mary Haworth, columnist, and King Features Syndicate; Dr. Rexford Hersey, University of Pennsylvania, as quoted in *New Techniques of Happiness*, by Albert Edward Wiggam, Wilfred Funk, Inc., 1948; Anne Heywood, for "Opportunities Unlimited," column, King Features Syndicate, N.Y., N.Y.; John Hancock Mutual Life Insurance Company; *Journal* of *Applied Psychology*, Washington, D.C., for "Selected Factors which Influence Job Preferences," by C. E. Jurgensen, December, 1947; Dr. Verne Kallejian, psychologist, Institute of Industrial Relations, University of California at Los Angeles; *Ladies Home Journal* for High School Career Series "Secretarial Work"; Lederle Laboratories Division, American Cyanamid Company; and the *Chevron*, for "That Man in the Office"; *Life*; Life Office Management Association; Los Angeles Merchants and Manufacturers Association; McGraw-Hill for *You Must Relax*, by Edmund Jacobson, M.D.; *Mill and Factory*; *Mechanical Engineering*; National Broadcasting Company; National Secretaries Association; *The New York Times*; *The Office*; *Office Executive*, published by National Office Management Association; *Office Management*; Mrs. Emily Post, Emily Post Institute, New York City; *Power*; Random House, for *The Disenchanted*, by Budd W. Schulberg, 1950; Records Management Association of New York; Research Institute of America, Inc., for *How to Handle Women*, 1953; Rohrer, Hibler, and Replogle, Cleveland; Seraphic Secretaries of America; Survey Research Center, Institute for Social Research, University of Michigan, Ann Arbor, for *Productivity, Supervision and Morale in an Office Situation*, Part I, by Daniel Katz, Nathan Maccoby, and Nancy C. Morse, 1950; Dr. J. Edward Stieglitz, Women's Bureau, U.S. Department of Labor, for statement in *Hiring Older Women*; J. Walter Thompson Company, New York City; John S. Tomajan, President, Washburn Company, Worcester, Mass., as quoted in *Individual Initiative in Business*, Harvard University Press, 1950; Transcription Supervisors' Association of New York; *Trends*, publication of Record Controls, Inc.; Muriel Tsvetkoff, General Manager, Better Business Bureau, San Francisco; Professors Otto von Mersing of Harvard University and Stephen Kegeles, of Boston, for survey made with Soundscriber Corporation; *Wall Street Journal*; Dr. Albert Edward Wiggam; *Woman's Home Companion*, for "To Do More Work with Less Fatigue," by Judith Chase Churchill, November, 1952.

Also to many manufacturers of business machines including: R. C. Allen Business Machines, Inc.; Audograph Company; Smith Corona, Inc.; Ralph C. Coxhead Corp.; Dictaphone Corporation; Ditto, Inc.; Thomas A. Edison, Inc.; International Business Machines Corp.; National Cash Register Company; Remington Rand, Inc.; Royal Typewriter Co., Inc.; Soundscriber Corporation; Underwood Corporation; Webster-Chicago Corp.

Preface

The first question any thinking person asks concerning a new book is, what is its purpose?

Several girls read the manuscript of *Success and Satisfaction in your Office Job*. An accounting clerk told us, "There's nothing in this book I couldn't have written myself. It's exactly the way things happen in my work." Her tone was slightly disparaging, as if to imply that it doesn't take much ability to report what's going on every day.

But unconsciously, she paid the book its highest compliment. For her remark assured us that we had apparently succeeded in our purpose in writing this book—to share with the more than six million women in offices throughout the United States the knowledge that their experiences and problems are universal. Those who attain success and satisfaction do so not because they have some mythically perfect job with ideal conditions. In the large majority of cases, they create their own happy and successful job environment.

The second question might be, what effect will the book have upon its readers? A secretary who also read the manuscript gave the following reaction: "The secretarial school from which I was graduated was tops in teaching us skills. We were drilled in diction, poise and telephone techniques. But when I started working in an office, things were different. The business world wasn't waiting for me to show off my accomplishments. In spite of my excellent training, I couldn't cope realistically with some of the situations that confronted me."

This secretary expressed the need for a book to provide "how to" techniques for adjusting attitudes and developing personality traits that lead to satisfaction in your job. We hope this book will fill that need. The step from satisfaction to success—whether measured in terms of financial reward or prestige or an opportunity for self-expression—is a short one. If reading this book puts you on that path, our hopes will be fulfilled.

Success and Satisfaction in Your Office Job creates positive attitudes and motivates readers to self-improvement. To make the book completely effective, companies may wish to provide training as a transition from reading to actual practice in skills. For this purpose a "Manual for Upgrading and Training Office Employees," closely coordinated with the contents of the book, is available without charge to executives.

A Discussion Outline is supplied to business schools that use *Success and Satisfaction in Your Office Job*, in their teaching.

Letters regarding the supplementary aids, if addressed to the authors, care of the publisher, will be forwarded for action.

E. B. AND R. L. L.

Contents

CHAPTER I

Success and Satisfaction

"You can make your own job if you work in an office," Meg Skillman answered when asked why she had chosen office work as a career.

Pressed for an explanation, she said, "Of course, some girls just put their hours in and take their pay. But if you are really interested, office work opens all kinds of doors for you. Not only can you change the job to suit your abilities, but you can also get real satisfaction out of working."

Office work is the most flexible of all occupations for women. The government lists twenty-five major classifications of office jobs that predominantly employ women. They include the more widely known occupations of bookkeeper, clerk, stenographer, typist, and secretary. In addition, want ad columns advertise for administrative assistants, analysts, billers, checkers, research librarians, supervisors, switchboard operators, bank tellers, and many others.

But these classifications do not tell the whole story. A typist's work ranges from simple copying to reproducing complicated statistical tables and manuscripts. Jobs in bookkeeping include positions from clerk to head bookkeeper in charge of a department. Machine operators may use relatively simple machines to record only one type of data or may perform involved computations on special machines.

Stenographers may take dictation or operate dictating machines. Others become specialists in foreign languages, legal or medical work. Secretaries may handle business details in addition to stenographic duties, or may have their own secretary or stenographer to do routine work for them.

Many an enterprising girl hired for a certain job in a short time transforms her prescribed work into something entirely different.

A textile company put into effect a job evaluation system for office employees. The girls were interviewed, observed at their work, and written job descriptions of their duties prepared. These job descriptions were approved by their respective supervisors or bosses.

After a year, the job descriptions were reviewed. In a number of instances, the girls who held the jobs had so changed their duties that the descriptions were obsolete.

A clerk took over placing small purchase orders independently because her boss felt she sometimes "shopped around" more carefully than he had time to do. A bookkeeper added drawing up a trial balance to her duties. A stenographer gradually assumed complete preparation of a progress report which originally had to be dictated to her.

These girls had their jobs "bustin' out all over" with added responsibilities. They had made their own jobs—created a special niche for themselves in their offices.

MAKING YOUR OWN JOB IN OFFICE WORK

Since we obviously select office work because it appeals to us, it would seem natural that we should be happy with our jobs and find them a source of satisfaction. Many of us do.

Glamour Magazine asked "the girl with the vital job,"— the mail girl, messenger, page, receptionist, clerk, office machine operator, stenographer, secretary, telephone operator— "What are the six most satisfying elements of your work?" They listed:

The chance it offers to help others;
The opportunity it gives to learn;
The contact it provides with people;
The challenge that it brings;
The variety of duties it calls for;
The worthwhile accomplishments it represents.

The editorial comment to these girls was:

You are the wise ones who have the right perspective. You are the far-seeing ones who, while recognizing the importance of salary and all the other individually undeniably serious considerations still regard them as less permanent sources of contentment than your first six values. This is because you know a job is more than just a way to make a living. It is also a way to live fully and wisely and well.

"Challenge of diversified work and of responsibility" was the top reason for enthusiasm cited by 45 per cent of the New York Chapter members of the National Secretaries Association in a study made by the Underwood Corporation.

On the other hand, a survey published by *The Office* magazine discloses that more than 25 per cent of a thousand office girls, interviewed in thirty-nine states, expressed some dissatisfaction with their jobs. This would seem to indicate that there is a definite need for a guide to positive action.

This book aims to provide such a guide by showing how you can:

1. Make a study of your personality as it functions in the office.
2. Build pride in your appearance, your work and your company.
3. Strive for recognition of your abilities and derive pleasure from a sense of accomplishment.
4. Learn to work at a relaxed pace, without too much tension.

5. Appreciate the value of tact.
6. Practice cooperation to cut corners.
7. Plan with a purpose.
8. Find adventure in initiative.
9. Let machines help you develop.
10. Understand how to solve problems.

SO MUCH A PART OF YOUR LIFE

You may stop to wonder, "Why should I devote so much effort to my job?"

The first incentive for you is that the office is such an important part of your life. You've heard people say, "I'm *giving* the best years of my life *to* my job." Actually, they mean, "I'm *living* the best years of my life *in* my job." In office work, we never quite know when work ends and our personal life begins. If you make your work live, you make the most of your job.

Our major decisions are often dictated by our job. To a considerable extent, work determines where you live. Perhaps you'd like to move to Florida, or southern California, or to some other vacation spot. But you feel you couldn't get as good a job there as the one you now have, or you might miss the people you work with. So you remain where you are.

Office work may exert such a powerful hold on us that it diverts us from an intended career in another field. This is likely to happen when a girl takes an office job for the purpose of saving up for training in one of the professions. After a year or two she finds office work a fascinating career in itself.

Take Muriel Tsvetkoff, Manager of the Better Business Bureau in San Francisco. In school, Muriel studied voice and piano, sang in a church choir, and saved $250 for advanced musical training. The tuition rates at the music school which she had chosen greatly exceeded her savings. This didn't dampen her ambition, though. She enrolled with a noted piano teacher in Berkeley and took a secretarial job with the Oakland Better Business Bureau to finance her studies.

Business gradually replaced music in her affections. Her secretarial job became an end rather than a means. From Oakland she moved across the bay to the San Francisco Bureau as the manager's secretary. On his retirement a few years later, the directors looked for a replacement. Their choice was Muriel.

The influence of the office extends into our outside social life. The people we meet on our way to and from the office are usually associates from our own company and other organizations. Our lunch dates are with those doing similar work. We go shopping with the girls for clothes. The styles we pick are prescribed by office standards.

Our speech is neither the slang of the factory nor the vocabulary of the college professor. It is straightforward and to the point—the language of business.

Our life may come to center so much around our business activities that we find ourselves lonely if through unforeseen circumstances we give up our job.

Lillian had been head of the centralized filing department for a large corporation when her aunt died and left her a substantial legacy. So Lillian resigned and took a cruise around the world. When she returned, she furnished a bachelor apartment, hunting up antiques with the same efficiency that formerly characterized her office performance. For a while, friends from the office came to admire her acquisitions. They brought the latest office gossip and accounts of what was going on. But gradually they drifted away, as office events became more and more remote to Lillian since she no longer participated in them. Lillian tried charity work, but as a newcomer felt herself outside the established "cliques."

Now Lillian is again working in an office, even though she

doesn't need the money. She gets satisfaction out of her accomplishments, and her office friends make her apartment a rendezvous. Lillian's days are again crowded with purposeful activity.

Office environment affects our home life. Office problems are the subject of our conversation at the supper table, or at least they influence our mood. Much has been written about the effect of a happy home life on a person's career. The reverse is also true. If the boss has praised us for a job well done, we tell mother that she has fixed a fine supper for us, or we surprise our husband by picking up some delicacy he likes on the way home.

AN OFFICE JOB HAS MANY ADVANTAGES

The second reason why it's worth while to make the most of your job is that you have a head start to success and satisfaction in office work. An office job has many advantages.

DIGNITY

Office work gives us a sense of dignity. It has prestige. In companies where the factory and offices are located in the same building, girls are even willing to take less money, if necessary, to transfer from production work to the office. They will sacrifice skills learned on the bench, and take new training, to qualify for desk jobs.

Donald and Eleanor Laird report in *Practical Business Psychology* that many factory workers "skimp and save so their children can take courses to prepare for office work. Parents are motivated to make these sacrifices because office workers enjoy greater prestige. The factory parent whose son or daughter works in an office basks in reflected glory."[1]

[1] Donald A. & Eleanor C. Laird. *Practical Business Psychology.* New York: The Gregg Publishing Company, 1951.

OPPORTUNITY

The traditional entering wedge for higher jobs is still the secretarial route. Other channels for advancement revealed by the Division of Research of the Harvard Business School which studied the Radcliffe Management Training Program for Women, are:

1. Secure specific training. The type of training most consistently mentioned by executives was the use of figures—the fundamentals of accounting and statistics.
2. Start with a company while it is new and small. Two women who had attained unusual positions in their companies, the general sales manager of a china manufacturing company and the personnel director of a large Chicago manufacturing firm, both attributed their rise to the fact that they had grown with the company. They had had an opportunity in the early days to learn all phases of operation.
3. Enter the more "creative" fields, such as magazine publishing, merchandising, promotion, public relations.

STEADY EMPLOYMENT

Office work provides steady employment. Figures gathered by the Bureau of the Census show that of all women who are working, the highest percentage with long service—those who have been with the same employer for ten years or more—are in the office group.

UTILIZES EDUCATION

An office enables you to make the most effective use of your training and education. A poll conducted among personnel directors of companies in the New York area showed that for general office work 38 per cent preferred high school graduates with business school training, against 26 per cent who preferred college graduates with business school training. For those who have college training, an article in the house organ of the Ethyl Corporation suggests a word of caution. "Most men will quickly hire a girl who has a sparkling personality and plenty of eye-appeal, and are usually impressed with even a smattering of college education, but oddly enough, unless these qualities are kept in the background, they soon become sources of irritation in a working situation."

The "ideal office girl," as picked by one representative group of business men, does not have college training. She is twenty-five years old, a brunette, single, and a business school graduate.

HELPS FIND A HUSBAND

A woman is more likely to find a husband in the office than in any other career. The American Institute of Family Relations in Los Angeles conducted a survey on the marriage prospects of fifteen occupations. The "prospects" were rated in the following order: (1) secretary, (2) actress, (3) bookkeeper, (4) stenographer, (5) journalist, (6) sales clerk, (7) hostess, (8) buyer, (9) nurse, (10) lawyer, (11) teacher, (12) dietician, (13) librarian, · (14) social worker, (15) physician.

At an all male college there is considerable turnover among the office force of some thirty girls. The office manager has no difficulty hiring replacements, however, in spite of the moderate salaries the college pays. "The girls just want to catch an engineer for a husband," is the way he accounts for it. "Man-hunting has been especially good since the G.I. Bill of Rights brings older men to the College. Graduate students and the younger professors are also good marital prospects."

COMMON INTERESTS WITH HUSBAND

An office job brings you closer to understanding your husband's interests if you are married. You may not be in the same line of work, but you keep in touch with what is going on in the business world.

CONTACT WITH THE BOSS

"I want to work for a man boss!" Girls in offices are practically unanimous on this point. A survey made by the *Woman's Home Companion* discloses that women prefer men as bosses because men make them feel they are working *with* rather than *for* a person.

It is fortunate that most bosses are men. For just as women prefer men bosses, the men prefer women for office jobs. And that's not because they like having women around, but because, as shown by the Minnesota Clerical Test, women are naturally best equipped for stenography, typing, filing, and the intricate details of office work.

Office work is a natural form of expression for a woman. She is contented in her role for the same reason that a woman running her home is contented. Dorothy Herbst writes in *The Office Economist* that the office woman is "working on the creative level—manipulating her environment to bring order out of disorder. She finds satisfaction in a job where she knows that her natural abilities are important."

The office girl "keeps house for the nation's business," according to the tribute made in a full-page magazine advertisement of the John Hancock Mutual Life Insurance Company:

You make a phone call, and it's her voice that answers.

You dictate a letter, and it's she who transcribes it.

You need a speech that somebody made two or three years ago . . . Or was it four? . . . Or was it a magazine article? You can't recall, but she can, and has it on your desk in twenty minutes.

Who is this girl who turns up wherever business is done, remembering what you forget, doing what you haven't time to do, making the nation's offices as bright and orderly as a well-kept kitchen?

The personnel records say she's Miss Jones, secretary; Mrs. Brown, receptionist; Miss Perry, file clerk; Miss Hoyt, accounting machine operator. They tell you she's 21 or 43, that she's worked here and there, that she went to this or that school.

Maybe the records should tell you more.

Perhaps they should mention that Miss Jones has an invalid mother, and never lets her problem show in the face you see from nine to five.

Perhaps they should say that Mrs. Brown is supporting a son in college, that Miss Perry practices shorthand during her lunch hours, that Miss Hoyt is studying business administration at night.

And where is that card that tells you that work in America is a happier thing because Miss Jones is there, and Mrs. Brown, and Miss Perry, and Miss Hoyt, bringing some softening touch into the places where jobs are done?

Take a letter, Miss Jones, "To whom it may concern: Thanks for your help. Thanks for spelling better than I do, and for knowing what I don't. Thanks for remembering when a collective noun takes a singular verb, and for wearing a flower on rainy mornings, and for being cheerful when I am not, and for knowing how to work hard and still be human. Thanks for being everywhere that a bright mind, a willing hand, and a pleasant way are needed."

Mail it to yourself, Miss Jones. Sign it, "Very sincerely yours."

CHAPTER II

Plot Your Personality Profile

IF YOU have your personality analyzed by a psychologist, you take tests that evaluate your character. He plots your scores on a chart and connects the points with lines. He calls this chart a profile of your personality.

Borrowing from this idea, we can periodically "score" our selves in our own minds. We can mentally plot a chart or picture to visualize our personality profile.

THE TYPE OF WORK WE DO

The first point to determine is whether we are doing the type of office work for which we are best fitted. In other words, do we prefer paper, people or places?

Office jobs offer all three in varying degrees.

A thirty-year old clerk was unhappy because she had not been promoted to section head. She had handled every clerical job in the department, was considered efficient and had reached top grade. "If anyone knows all the forms and procedures, I do," she asserted. "What's more, I've never asked anyone for a bit of help and I've always minded my own business."

The office manager explained to her that the position of section head meant dealing with people, rather than a knowledge of paper work. He cited her reluctance to mix with those about her, and even the fact that she ate lunch alone.

"But," he advised her, "you have an unusually keen comprehension of records and systems, and a logical mind. Why not take a few courses in statistics, in order to be prepared in case there is an opening as an analyst in our marketing and sales division?" She followed his advice and now has a job in which she is happy because it entails analytical thinking with a minimum of contact with others.

Some people want a job that does not tie them to one place. Office messengers or guides who conduct tours of large factories belong in this category. Many jobs require research in libraries, or visiting other companies for information. Some accounting offices send girls along with the CPA's to their client's organizations. The top traveling job probably is working for an executive who must take a secretary along on his trips.

If you decide that you are not in your proper niche, it doesn't mean that you should give your job up right away and seek another. But you can do two things:

1. In "making your own job" you can guide your present work along the lines of your personality inclination. If you like people, for example, make the most of your contacts with people.

2. Be on the lookout for the kind of job, either in your own organization or elsewhere, that best utilizes your personality characteristics.

THE PART PERSONALITY PLAYS

Business executives are increasingly aware of the relationship between personality and job success and satisfaction. Evidence of this is an advertisement in *The New York Times*:

PERSONALITY CLASHES

are responsible for more discharges and "quits" than any other single factor in employment relations. Recent studies indicate that jobs lost through personality difficulties range from 75% to 90%.

And strangely enough, physical environment—while important—was but a minor consideration in many of the cases studied. Air-conditioning, good lighting, commodious quarters and attractive furnishings have their place and their effect on good morale, but—once again —it is only part of the total situation.

It is our feeling that the clearest air and the brightest light come from complete understanding of the needs of each individual as such—and that this can be accomplished only by continuous attention to the important task of providing able supervision and its end product— good teamwork.

(*Burns & Roe, Inc., Engineering Constructors*)

HOW TO ADAPT OUR PERSONALITY

Regardless of the type of work we do, it is inevitable that we must make adaptations in the office. Management can do its part by proper selection, placement, and supervision, as indicated in the advertisement just quoted, but the final responsibility for the effectiveness of our personalities rests with us as individuals.

Four suggestions to help accomplish this are:

1. We can't and shouldn't be continually concentrating on what we say and how we behave, on our ups and downs, our interaction with others, our adjustment to the boss. That would inhibit us, make us self-conscious.

2. We need not be concerned with every single personality trait we possess. Some traits do not affect our satisfaction or success as far as the office is concerned one way or the other. It is not pertinent whether a girl likes sports or prefers reading a book; whether she is somewhat shy or the life of the party.

3. We should be aware of the fact that our personalities change over a period of time. They are affected by the conditions under which we work, and the people we deal with. The sheepherder develops a slow-moving mental pattern. The

aviator is forced to think fast. A leisurely pace becomes part of the personality of the girl surrounded by the academic atmosphere of a small college. Trigger-like activity characterizes her sister who seeks adventure in a New York or Hollywood broadcasting studio.

4. We should watch particularly those traits which are accentuated in our work with others. Check yourself on the following qualities which are highlighted in office relationships.

CHECKPOINTS ON OFFICE PERSONALITY

ARE YOU DEPENDABLE?

We all want people to trust us. But to merit such trust, we must be dependable.

Martha was a typist assisting the treasurer's secretary, Miss Simpson. Martha's work was largely routine. Usually what was not finished one day could wait till the next.

One of her few specifically assigned tasks was to copy a statement that was mailed to the directors every Tuesday evening. The pencil copy of the statement ordinarily was on her desk the first thing Tuesday morning—giving her ample time to finish it.

On a certain Tuesday, however, some changes had to be made. The rough draft of the statement was not ready till after lunch. When five o'clock came, she had not completed the typing.

Martha had to take several busses if she went home by public conveyance. But conveniently she was able to share-ride with several others. When her companions were ready at five o'clock, she just left the final sheet of the statement in the typewriter, covered her machine, put the rest of the work in the desk, and went home.

Since Miss Simpson was in the treasurer's office at the time,

Martha didn't tell her about the unfinished work. Neither did she leave a note. It took considerable hunting before Miss Simpson located the statement under the typewriter cover. The treasurer decided right then and there that Martha couldn't be trusted with responsibility.

ARE YOU SELF-CONFIDENT?

Self-confidence is a mental habit or attitude. If you learn to do a thing well, you create confidence in your ability to continue to do it. You are confident of your ability to walk. If you fall, you don't decide that you can't walk any more.

In your job, you should acquire confidence in your skill, in spite of the fact that you may make occasional mistakes. The secretary to the editor of the *Ladies Home Journal* believes that "the most important qualification a girl can have is confidence—in herself and in her ability to produce."

ARE YOU ACCURATE?

Accuracy helps us to function smoothly. A survey of business men in Portland, Oregon, listed accuracy as one of the three most important traits they desired in office employees.

We may be inclined to make the excuse, "Oh, accuracy isn't my strong point. I'm a fast typist . . . and the two don't always go together."

Yet tests show that speed and accuracy usually go hand-in-hand. In a typewriting experiment, one group of beginners was told to emphasize accuracy, and another group to emphasize speed. After four months, the speed group typed thirty-eight words per minute. The accuracy group typed forty-five words— working for accuracy made them 18 per cent faster. The accuracy group also had only half as many errors.

Slow workers often are more careless than fast workers. What really happens is that most people are alternately both accurate and inaccurate.

Jean was in a stenography pool. Whenever she was called into the president's office for dictation, she did perfect work. But most of the time she typed reports. These were not immediately checked, but consolidated with other typing. Corrections were made by the supervisor of the stenographic pool when she read over the entire set of reports. She did not take time to trace the various girls who made the errors.

Jean did sloppy work on these reports simply because she would not be embarrassed by having her errors called to her attention—as was the case when she worked for the president. She was capable of accurate work when she felt it counted.

Accuracy is more important than speed. You may be asked how many words a minute you can type when you are hired or given a test. But this is seldom checked after you're on the job. Your mistakes, on the contrary, are detected every time you make them.

Are You a Perfectionist?

Perhaps you spend too much time on some jobs. You may be a perfectionist. Some girls are meticulous about erasures, even on a rough draft. Others insist on giving an exact figure, down to the last decimal, when an estimate or round figure is all that is called for.

Helen was asked to go to the library and copy half a dozen references on a new law. Instead, she came back with every single reference she could dig up—a half day's work. Most of these obscure references had no value for the purpose intended.

The saying, "What's worth doing is worth doing well," is often disproved in the office because of time limitations. Tailoring your work to the requirements of a job is good self-management.

ARE YOU FLEXIBLE?

You may be inclined to follow rigid patterns of behavior—the kind of person psychologists call "compulsive." A compulsive complains if someone sits at her desk or uses her office equipment, whether it inconveniences her or not. She has a place for everything, everything in its place, and a time when everything has to be done. To some extent this is desirable, but it can be overdone.

Miss Hart made it a point to stay and clean up every bit of work each day. Her co-workers considered her exemplary. Everyone admired her high standards of efficiency.

During the vacation period, a temporary girl replaced her. One day, her boss dictated a long report late in the afternoon. "We can send it out tomorrow," he added.

The substitute girl replied, "I'll be glad to do it tonight, but if tomorrow is time enough, I'll type it the first thing in the morning."

"That will be fine," he answered, and then with some reticence continued, "Miss Hart always finishes all her work the day I give it to her. Sometimes, I like to clean up my desk when I have time late in the day, even though it doesn't matter just when the work is typed. But because I know she'll insist on transcribing it, naturally I avoid overloading her." This boss had somewhat reluctantly adapted himself to his secretary's set ways.

Flexibility is part of the give and take of good office relations.

Ethel had a long report in her typewriter when her boss asked her if she would get out a short statement. She took out the report and did the statement right away.

"Not many girls would take out their typing in the middle of the page to be accommodating," her boss commented,

pleased that he would not be delayed. "Will you have to do it over?"

"No," Ethel reassured him, "I'll be careful to get it back in the same spot."

Are You "Bossy?"

"My chief records clerk is so efficient, she takes things right out of my hands," an office manager remarked approvingly. "One word from me, and she does as she pleases! And her way is invariably better than mine, too."

Some girls acquire this habit of dominating because, to a certain extent, they have to assert themselves if they want to get ahead in business. Many provide for parents and manage a home, which strengthens this tendency to "take over."

Business men praise such girls highly, and feel they couldn't get along without them. But, over a period of time, they also simultaneously come to resent them. As one boss put it, "I'd like to be right once in a while, too, or at least think I am!"

A major reason why so many attractive, intelligent girls with fine jobs never marry is that they develop the habit of "running with the ball." A boss in business may condone this practice, because after all he benefits by it. But it scares off prospective husbands!

Are You Emotionally Stable?

Do you have periods when you don't seem to accomplish anything? When you lose things? When your accounts don't balance? Starting right at nine o'clock, everything seems to go wrong.

Charting the emotions and moods of a group of employees of the Pennsylvania Railroad Company some years ago, Professor Rexford Hersey found that almost all showed regular cyclic swings, ranging from thirty-two to thirty-six days. For several weeks they felt better and better. They achieved more. They got along well with their fellow employees.

Then the graph would show a sharp drop. The people became irritable. Their work fell below normal. For from four to six days they would be in a low period. From this point on, they would start climbing again.

At first Dr. Hersey was convinced that each person had his own particular cycle length, and that is still his conclusion for many people. However, he has since found that the cycles are much more nearly alike for the majority of us than first appeared. This means that possibly we are worried and emotionally disturbed about 17 per cent of the time, pleasantly passive 78 per cent of the time, and exceptionally cheerful the other 5 per cent.

These emotional cycles are not affected by the natural cycles of a woman's body. If a woman is at a high point in her emotional cycle, she carries on her work with zest during her "period." If she is at a low point, she feels depressed and blue.

We should realize that such slumps, when they occur, are only temporary, and will pass. They should not be allowed to color our personality.

ARE YOU HYPER-SENSITIVE TO CRITICISM?

We are all subject to three types of criticism in our office relationships:

1. *Criticism of our personality.* This requires examining the motives of the person who finds fault with us. If these motives are well-intentioned, we should seriously take stock of ourselves.

2. *Criticism of our work.* This is merited if we are careless, inaccurate or unreliable. But we must discriminate if criticism is in reality a difference of opinion. We may be asked to draft a report, compose a letter, or do a piece of research. If we've

done our best and it doesn't meet with the desired approval, we should not be unduly sensitive.

A study made by the Research Institute of America reports that "when you are discussing her work, a woman is more likely to think you are discussing her. It is a rare woman who realizes that you can consider her work separate and apart from her as a person." As a general rule, women in the business world are likely to feel that they are on the defensive and have to prove themselves.

3. *Criticism of a situation in which we are the innocent by-standers.* Your employer requests some data you were supposed to type for a department head. You inform your boss that you haven't received the work yet. "I can't have such delays," he flares up, "I want you to see to it that the material is on my desk no later than three o'clock." Such criticism should disturb you least of all. It's directed at the department head, not at you.

ARE YOU ABLE TO CHANGE YOUR POINT OF VIEW?

Your job environment conditions you to certain viewpoints.

Grace had been associated for a number of years with the industrial relations director of a large corporation. Her boss was widely quoted for his broad-minded labor policies. Grace, as was to be expected, held opinions similar to his.

When her employer retired, Grace joined the industrial relations section of a college where she could utilize her background. One of her activities was to do research for arbitration cases. In this connection she had occasion to express her viewpoints on labor management problems to her department chairman—confident that he considered her quite liberal.

About a year after she had joined the staff, she was very much surprised when during a discussion, her department chairman observed, "You certainly have changed! Remember how biased you were when you first came here?"

You can guard against becoming one-sided by going to evening school, listening to provocative lectures, reading books. Your best barometer to judge whether you are developing a broad viewpoint is to get together with former office associates or friends whom you haven't seen for some time. Don't be disappointed if they seem dull or narrow-minded. You may be bored, but you will realize that in the interim you have mentally matured.

Are You Aware of the Profile You Present to Others?

Most of us are innately modest. We're under the impression that others don't pay much attention to our personality. Women, especially, feel that men do not have keen perception in this respect.

There's evidence to the contrary! One radio commentator claims he analyzes personality from the typewritten page:

"Wide margins indicate a high sensitivity of spirit, whereas narrow margins denote frugality. Average margins are a sign of intelligence and orderliness. A typist who strikes all letters with equal force is likely to be an unusually adaptable person with interest in her work. You can bank on a girl's being somewhat erratic, unpredictable, and easily distracted when deep impressions occur on the page as a result of pounding. Daintiness is reflected in one who shows a light touch but with every letter clearly defined. The adventurous girl, the one who'll pack a knapsack and explore a mountain peak will be found among typists whose idea is to get the message on paper, regardless of how it looks."

In a more profound manner, an executive quoted in *Glamour* magazine described his assistant:

"Of course, Alice is letter-perfect on the mechanical end—typing and shorthand. I realize she must have had excellent training to reach this high point of skill. But she seems to consider this just the beginning of her work. I couldn't remember all the things she quietly stepped in and took over for me—the letters she's composed and simply submitted for my approval, the smooth, diplomatic way the telephone calls are running, the way routine matters with customers are handled without my being called in at all. I haven't forgotten a meeting or been late for an appointment in six months. I don't think my memory's getting any better—it's simply that she's been on hand to remind me.

"I enjoy watching her learn the business. Some of her questions really tickle me—they're so perceptive. And when I find trade journals and books about the industry on her desk I know it's no accident. But with all this study and interest I particularly appreciate the fact that she doesn't tell everyone in the company how the business should be run. Especially me.

"She has a quality which, for lack of a better phrase, I think of as a strong sense of decorum. She knows when a situation calls for friendly informality and when it should be businesslike. I never have to warn her that she should be especially careful with a particular customer; and on the other hand she never seems resentful if I ask her to go get me a sandwich or dust off the desk.

"I like her because she has all the old-fashioned virtues—diligence, integrity, loyalty—in such an attractive, good-to-look-at modern form."

CHAPTER III

Put Pride in Your Performance

Suppose you question three girls about their work. The first one tells you indifferently, "I'm only a clerk." The second seems pleased with herself and asserts, "I make a good salary as an order clerk." The third glances up with enthusiasm and says, "It's my responsibility to see that the orders are properly processed—as quickly as possible. We have a lot of important customers to take care of!"

What distinguishes the comment of the third girl? She has pride—not only in her work, but in her company.

Pride is closely linked to job success and satisfaction. The Survey Research Center of the University of Michigan has made a study of clerical workers and their supervisors in the home office of the Prudential Insurance Company. They found that pride in the work group has a distinct relationship to work output. 33 per cent of the employees in the sections which had a high output showed pride in their group's activity. Only 10 per cent of the employees in low sections cared how their group stood in comparison with others.

Companies are now starting to instill pride right when the new employee is hired. Company handbooks captioned "Welcome to Smith and Adams," or "You and Your Job," make you feel part of the organization you are joining.

A wholesale house stresses to new employees the value of every single job in the company. "We make certain each girl as she is hired realizes that the work she will do is highly essential in some manner to assure prompt service to our retailers."

"File clerk" advertisements are becoming increasingly unpopular among skilled records clerks who consequently avoid them when seeking a new job. They feel that the title undervalues their vital role in the firm's functioning. *Trends*, the publication of Record Controls, Inc., reveals that new titles, to dignify the file clerk position are: librarian, archivist, records clerk, records assistant, consultant, attendant, examiner, manager, director, custodian.

It builds our self-esteem to refer to our title with pride. When a girl tells you, "I'm secretary to Mr. . . ." she does it with an air of distinction. She'll protest, too, if you ill-advisedly call her a stenographer. Even high school courses are listed as "secretarial studies." The New York State Employment Service has discontinued the stenographer job classification. And the New York Teacher-Clerks Association has requested the Board of Education to change their title to "school secretary." Mrs. Mary B. Keller, the president, explained, "the duties of school clerks are diversified and comprise many categories—statistician, accountant, receptionist, telephonist, typist, stenographer, secretary—even nurse! We maintain that 'school clerk' does not do justice to the position nor command the proper respect."

The National Broadcasting Company gets around the prejudice of hiring stenographers by classifying new recruits, fresh from school, as "junior secretaries." This gives them recognition, and at the same time preserves the prestige of secretaries with longer service.

THREE-DIMENSIONAL IMPRESSIONS

The impression you make on the job is a three-dimensional projection of your pride in your performance. People judge you by your personal appearance, the way you keep your office, desk or work place, and the work you turn out.

1. An office job offers you opportunity to appear at your best. The traditional tailored suit and crisp blouse worn by office girls is the outfit most frequently seen on motion picture stars—although the script could just as easily call for more glamorous styles. Polls of men indicate their first choice in a costume for a woman is "a suit in a becoming color."

The American office girl is also known for her meticulous grooming. Money spent for the beauty parlor and cosmetics is considered essential expense for "upkeep." The Bristol-Myers Company has just issued a handy pamphlet, *The Girl for the Job*, which has daily, weekly, monthly, semi-annual and annual grooming check lists for office girls. It tells us that "the personnel director, your boss and all the people you work with will be more likely to recognize you as a smart girl if you look and act the part—and this means being well groomed at all times. Good grooming is one of your biggest assets in the business world. Knowing you're at your best gives you the poise and self-confidence you need to put your best foot forward."

2. We set the stage for our performance by an impression of clean-cut efficiency in our office. Even though our own desks and tables are neat, we may have to contend with a boss such as Mr. Milgrim, the movie magnate, described in the book, *The Disenchanted*.[1]

The wide expanse of the Milgrim desk supported hundreds of items, pieces in an endless game played between Milgrim and Miss Dillon. He was always snatching things up and laying them down on the wrong pile. She was forever rearranging so the huge desk would not appear cluttered.

What counts most is not any individual desk, but the overall picture. It is easy to become accustomed to leaving papers,

[1] Budd W. Schulberg, *The Disenchanted*. New York: Random House, 1950.

books and supplies piled around us, on window sills, tables, chairs, and floor. It's good practice to call in a "consultant" from time to time—a girl friend from another department with a critical eye to help us see ourselves as others see us.

3. The appearance of your work reflects your attitude toward it. Your letters are you. Most bosses will give you permission to make corrections or do over a job if you tell them, "I like my work to look nice." The trouble is, we don't always remember that others will notice our work.

Louise was a fast but somewhat careless typist. Her letters had that "worked over" look that comes from too many erasures. One day she was put on a special campaign where she had to use a typewriter with a distinctive type. Since the machine was new to her, she had to go slow, with the result that her work improved. Several of the people who responded to the campaign added postscripts commending the attractive typing. Louise was delighted with these complimentary remarks. She began to take real pride in her typing.

EVERYONE HAS A ROLE TO PLAY

The average TV buyer seldom sees or thinks about the many thousand separate parts inside his television set. He's unaware that these parts are skillfully soldered together by hundreds of connections. Yet the performance of a television set and long-range satisfaction depend to a large extent upon the quality of the parts and the care with which they are assembled. Some parts of our job are equally unseen or unnoticed. But they contribute to the operation of our company. No matter what you do, remember you make a contribution or you would not be there.

You should know the significance of your job. An example given by a steel corporation executive was quoted in *Office Executive,* the official publication of the National Office Management Association: "In one of our plants a few years ago," he said, the head of one of our office departments heard a lady typist say, 'For years I have been writing these reports about the daily, weekly, monthly and yearly ingot production. What in the world is an ingot?' "

Perhaps you will retort that your company doesn't do too much to let you know where you fit in. That may be so. But perhaps you never thought of taking advantage of the opportunities and obvious sources of information offered to you. Ask yourself:

Do I carefully read the notices on the bulletin board, or do I just glance to see when the next holiday is announced?

Do I read the factual information in the house organ, catalog, the sales brochures, the technical magazines, put out by the company?

Do I use the company library?

Do I ask in department stores whether they carry the product my company is making?

If my vacation takes me to a place where branch offices are located, have I ever asked whether I might wisely pay a visit there?

Do I occasionally ask my boss, when he is not busy, the purpose of the statements I work on, the records we keep?

Have I taken the trouble to find out how an order for our product is obtained, how it is filled, what happened before and after it came to my desk?

Do I have any idea of the value and importance of the different items I post in the ledger, enter in files, or write about in correspondence?

Have I shown any interest in the work that others are doing? (But here you must be careful not to appear "snoopy.")

Most bosses expect us to have a certain amount of curiosity about our company. A section head in an insurance office put it this way: "I would refuse to take on a girl in my department unless, when I showed her regulations, directives or the company handbook, she would be sufficiently interested to ask whether she could take home some of the material to get acquainted with it before starting to work."

YOU ARE A PRESS AGENT.

A sales manager had a reputation for his brilliant presentations. His talks were widely published in trade journals. Yet his over-all "job performance" was not an asset to the company. When a big order was ready to break, he would jump in to close it, belittling the salesman in the territory. He was continually critical of the work of other departments. He openly attacked administrative policies.

We've all had occasion to observe such men. They only have pride in their own accomplishments. But pride in "job performance" has broader implications. It includes loyalty to the people associated with us, and particularly to the company as a whole.

Most of us do not consciously set out to disparage the reputation of our company. We just "muff" our lines—blurt out confidential information without realizing what we are saying.

A girl admired the napkins as she lunched at the home of a friend. "They're made by your company," the hostess answered, mentioning an old-established linen concern. "They ought to be good. I paid a dollar apiece for them!"

"What?" the girl exclaimed, "we sell them to the wholesaler for 35¢!" The disillusioned hostess may conceivably not buy this type of napkin again.

Costs and prices are often inadvertently divulged. Labor and material going into the manufacture of an article may cost only a relatively small sum, yet the article has to sell for six to eight times this amount to cover the overhead, commission, advertising, and scores of other items.

Not only must certain information be kept confidential but we must be watchful of impressions we unwittingly may create.

Kathleen, a typist in the office of the treasurer, had access to the salaries and confidential data about the executives. Nothing would induce her to tell even her own family the facts and figures she had in her head.

One day at a party discussion centered around the car which Mr. Williams, the vice president for sales, had just purchased. "Thank goodness, he doesn't run around in an old-fashioned model like the controller," one of the men commented.

"The controller can afford a new car better than Mr. Williams," Kathleen rose to the controller's defense unguardedly. It was easy for the others to draw some conclusions about the respective salaries of the two men.

If we listen in on conversations in the bus or subway, the chit-chat at the beauty parlor, the confidences exchanged between office girls over a ten o'clock cup of coffee, we find the company often comes out a poor second. Most of the derogatory remarks are thoughtless. Perhaps a girl is irked by some trivial incident. But the public forms its opinion about our company by what we say, just as it condemns an otherwise good play because a critic has pointed up a few minor flaws.

Pride in our performance calls for going out of our way to make a good impression.

Mr. Hamilton, president of a bank, was lunching with an investment broker, when the conversation turned to a certain aspect of loans.

"I've covered that in a booklet I've recently written called

Learning About Loans," the banker informed the broker. "I'll send you a copy if you want it."

Several months later, Mr. Hamilton had an appointment at the broker's office. The first thing he noticed among the books on the table beside the executive's desk was a copy of Learning About Loans. A public-relations minded secretary had placed it there.

A strategic job in many organizations is the receptionist at the employment desk. The editors of *Factory* magazine reported about a girl they observed that she was brusque, unsmiling, sharp-voiced and scolded five men for failing to answer questions on the application form. She did not call up waiting men to go to the interviewing office in the order in which they had completed applications. She held a personal conversation while the men waited. She commented to a messenger, "Some of these guys are awful jerks." New employees will not have a favorable impression of this company!

The receptionist in a doctor's office said, "I have to be particularly conscious of the way I make appointments over the telephone when patients are in the room. The doctor is a very busy man. But we don't want the patients to feel they will be rushed—that he doesn't give each one sufficient time when they come here."

Finally, remember if you should be looking for another job, don't run down your present boss or your present company. Your prospective employer will judge your future loyalty to his organization by the respect you show for the job you are leaving.

CHAPTER IV

The Road to Recognition

So FAR, we have discussed success and satisfaction in our job, and the personality factors by which we can achieve these objectives. Since these are our goals, what road should we travel to reach them—the well-paved highway, the road with scenery, or the shortest route to our destination? You undoubtedly want a road with all three advantages. Then you'll qualify your choice by adding, "That isn't always possible. The well-paved highway may lead to where I'm going, but it runs through flat, monotonous country." Or, "The road with scenery is winding and takes longer."

That's how it is with recognition. Sometimes you get financial recognition. You might compare this to the direct, paved highway. Money is the most logical reward for your efforts.

Or your job may not pay so much, but you are compensated by prestige, status, "social" recognition—the scenery that makes the trip pleasant.

More important than the well-paved highway or the scenery is the knowledge that the road is a means to an end. In the office, your ultimate goal is recognition of your ability. Of course, commensurate pay or status often coincide with appreciation of ability. But there are other times when you feel you are being side-tracked, just not getting anywhere financially. That's when you'll have to keep in mind that it doesn't matter how fast you're going, or whether you're on a detour of disappointment. It's the direction you're headed for that counts.

FINANCIAL RECOGNITION

"I got a raise today!" is exciting news. There's no denying that money means something to most of us. Soldiers at the front, for instance, wanted their pay regularly. Sometimes the paymaster had to inch up to the trenches. The GI's took their money and then handed it right back to be put in the safe at the base. It boosted their morale just to see the actual cash.

The extra dollars in a pay check are welcomed. But the real reason the raise is important is that it represents recognition. Sherman Billingsley of New York's Stork Club started the popular gesture of sending gifts to tables of his guests because he couldn't get around to everyone personally. Gifts let the customer know that he is recognized as an individual. A raise is a similarly individual gesture.

Sometimes a boss tells a girl in person she is slated for a raise. But even if he doesn't, she knows that he knows of her work when the raise comes through.

Unfortunately, sometimes we conclude that a raise is the only way that appreciation can be shown. Many a boss realizes those who work for them deserve more money, but he must abide by the company's established system of salary progression. For various reasons companies cannot always make their salary policy public. You may feel frustrated because you don't know when a raise is forthcoming or how you should go about getting it.

Office employees in half-a-dozen large companies in northern New Jersey, all of which had well-defined wage policies, held these misconceptions:

"I guess my salary is left to the discretion of my supervisor."

"Salaries seem to vary between persons in the same type of work—it depends on experience and ability."

"Salaries are on a personal approach basis—you talk to the boss directly."

"Yes, we get raises, but I'm vague about how."

So, even if you have doubts, don't let a delay in getting a raise discourage you from doing your best. A raise won't materialize more quickly because you fret about it. And your discontented attitude will affect your work to the extent that you handicap yourself for future advancement.

In some organizations where a rigid pay schedule exists, you may have a considerate boss who tries to make up to you in other ways to express his appreciation of your efforts. He may be liberal about "time off." He may pay you for personal work done outside of office hours. He may recommend your promotion to another department, even if it means he is depriving himself of an efficient employee. Too often we take such gestures for granted when in reality they are meant to reward us.

Pay differentials between employees who are equally matched may undermine morale unless we take positive action. Neta describes such a situation:

"Last Friday, we all got a raise in our company. Mine was for two dollars. You'd think I would be happy about it. But I'm not!

"I was hired a year ago, right after I was graduated from high school. In September, they hired Janice. She was in my senior class, but didn't have as high marks as I did. She had been to the shore for the summer. That's how she happened to start work later.

"When Janice came, they had an opening in the stenography pool that paid three dollars more than my job. This puts Janice in a higher bracket. When our raises came through last week, her bracket got a three dollar increase, against my two dollars. That puts her four dollars ahead of me.

"It's not the company's fault that I took the clerical job. But it doesn't seem right, either, that I should be getting four dollars less than Janice."

Girls like Neta may let such a grievance rankle for months, interfering with good job performance. Meanwhile, Neta's supervisor is wondering what's wrong with the girl's attitude. Both for her own job happiness and for the good morale of the group, Neta should confide in her supervisor to see if she can't be promoted to a different type of work. Only, if the transfer doesn't immediately materialize, Neta shouldn't let her present work slide in the interim. That would irrevocably shut the door to advancement.

Being too pay-conscious can block you off from interesting possibilities.

Carol was chief accounts payable clerk, when her entire department was reorganized under an IBM set-up. A supervisory job in the new department was offered to Carol, at a few dollars less than her current salary. The office manager made it clear that this was in no way a reflection on her ability, but merely necessary to keep salaries equalized. He assured her that as soon as the system was fully functioning, opportunities would develop for someone of her capabilities.

Carol indignantly refused. She left the company, and tried three or four jobs over a period of a year before she found something half-way suitable. Meantime, the supervisory job had been given to one of the girls who originally worked for Carol. The system had grown way beyond original estimates. Carol's former assistant was given increasing responsibilities and was getting more than Carol had ever earned.

Sometimes it's worth while to sacrifice a present pay advantage for future opportunity.

Jane was both secretary to the personnel director and a personnel interviewer. When her boss became vice president for personnel, he needed a full-time secretary, and offered the job to Jane. It was rated higher than her present position.

Jane, however, liked interviewing. She preferred personnel work as a career, and stayed at the lower salary. The satisfaction she got out of her job was the determining consideration.

Pay is less important to women than job security. A girl who was the receptionist in a dentist's office said, "I picked this job because you can be sure people will always need dental work. My sister was a clerk in a pencil factory. She made more than I did, but then the company moved away. My job has security!" It developed during the conversation that her sister had almost immediately found another clerical job. It was pointed out to this dental assistant that the skill acquired in office work is security in itself—it can be transferred to almost any type of industry or business.

Just how highly security is valued was evident in the case of a college graduate who had a job with a welfare agency. She liked the contacts and the people with whom she was associated, and the pay was more than she thought she was capable of earning. But she was on a *per diem* basis. Although she had been called in steadily for six days a week over a period of two years, she was still concerned about the permanence of her job. She confessed she would gladly have accepted less money if she could have been assured of her status.

The biggest financial headache, both for women in offices and for the management, is the publicity given to "equal pay for equal work."

A woman accountant feels slighted because she is doing exactly the same work as her male associates—at less pay. The clients of the CPA firm with which she is connected praise her fine work. But they still insist on a man to take charge of their audits. This is an instance where a company itself wants to put a woman on equal basis with men, but where public sentiment is against it. In an office, a woman may do all the research in connection with labor negotiations, but she can't go down in the shop and command the respect of the laborers as a man does. Every type of business or service has analogous situations. The work done by men and women may be similar in content, but it carries more authority when performed by a man.

To make your job relations more satisfying, you have to look this matter squarely in the face and ask yourself: "Am I personally discriminated against, or does my company, in general, differentiate between men and women?" In the majority of instances, you will find the problem is not personal. All over the country, it is still only in isolated cases that women in offices receive men's pay, although the trend is growing.

Instead of striving to attain the status of men, be content by doing the best a woman can do. When a woman accepts her job from that angle, she sometimes discovers unexpected possibilities for "the woman's touch" that were not apparent to her when she concentrated on her competition with men. That's why secretarial work is so rewarding. You don't compete with men, and your natural attributes are at their best advantage.

Money is an obvious and direct measure of recognition. But, as has already been indicated in some of the above instances, dollars and cents in the pay envelope are usually not of primary significance to women. This is borne out by a study made by C. E. Jurgensen on what factors are mentioned most frequently as having an important bearing on job satisfaction.[1] With women, pay was *ninth* on the list.

SOCIAL RECOGNITION

If we came to work each day, sat in an office by ourselves, added figures or typed, and saw no one, we wouldn't be able to

[1] C. E. Jurgensen. "Selected Factors Which Influence Job Preferences," in *Journal of Applied Psychology*, December, 1947.

stand it indefinitely, no matter what the size of the pay check. Office work is stimulating because we are in contact with people. In fact, office workers are "in the family," according to Dr. Ordway Tead.

Why is the secretarial job so highly prized? The actual typing, stenography and record keeping are much the same no matter where performed. But the secretary has contact with men of importance. She feels she does not work for her boss— she represents him. She "runs interference."

Marge, the secretary to the chief counsel of a food corporation, was looking for a new job. "I know it's ridiculous," she acknowledged, "I can't get anywhere near the money I'm making with Mr. Hemingway. But he doesn't give me an opportunity to do things for him."

Then she described the set-up. Her office was several doors away from that of the counsel's. She couldn't see his callers. He answered the telephone himself unless he was tied up in conference. Marge couldn't stand by with any information he might want as he talked on the phone. She couldn't service him in the hundred little ways that only good secretaries can anticipate. She was shut out of his office life.

How does your boss show you that he considers you "in the family?" Here are some answers gathered to this question:

"If I've been out, or on a vacation, he always tells me, 'We've missed you while you were away.' "

"Our supervisor's desk is at the front of the department. Everyone would see you if you went up there with a problem. So, if you tell him you have a personal matter to discuss, he'll let you come into the conference room during lunch hour. Privacy is as essential in the office on certain occasions as it is in the home."

"I had to go home Tuesday because of a cold. Thursday

morning my boss phoned me and told me not to come in till Monday. Wasn't that considerate?"

"Even if he's rushed, our office manager always stops at our desks to say 'Good morning.'"

"If we make a special effort to get out some work, the section head takes a few minutes at the end of the day to say he appreciates what we've done."

Above all, a boss shows he considers you "in the family" when by his actions he indicates that both he and you are working for the same employer—the company. John S. Tomajan, President of The Washburn Company, describes how he acquired this attitude.

"In my earlier days," he said, "I was relating to the sales manager how I had met a crisis. One of the girls had done something I did not like. I told her so. She replied that the former office manager had never objected. Instantly I put her in her place by retorting that she was now working for me, no longer for him. To my great embarrassment, instead of handing me an orchid, the sales manager smiled and said, 'Well, John, that was surely one way of handling that situation. But, you know, as a matter of fact, the young lady worked neither for your predecessor nor for you. She, just like you and me, works for the Washburn Company.'"

SOCIAL SYMBOLS

In a Chicago office, a swinging door separated the section where top executives' offices were located. Secretaries behind the "swinging door" considered themselves to have a higher social rank in the office, despite the fact that some people on the so-called "wrong" side of the door had more responsible jobs or got higher pay.

Sometimes we attach great importance to the kind of desk or chair certain people have, or the time they go to lunch, or to other outward symbols of distinction. Yet it's foolish to concern ourselves with such trifles, because they may be purely incidental.

Miss Manning had for years been the school clerk, with her desk in the principal's office. When the principal retired, her successor asked her to have her desk moved into the anteroom. Miss Manning was miserable. She felt this was a demotion after all her years of service.

Later she learned that the new principal, a younger man, was practically in awe of her precise New England dignity. "I like to smoke, and was positive Miss Manning would disapprove. She makes me feel like a little boy who's been sent to the principal's office for being bad. That's why I thought it would be better for both of us if she had her own office outside."

There is no basis to believe that people "rate" because they have their name on the door, or have a glass top for their desk, or eat from one to two o'clock. One executive approves of certain practices, another does not. Intrinsically such distinctions are meaningless.

Social status, the sense of "being in the family," pleasant working conditions, are integral factors in office life. But we undermine the satisfaction which our social relationships should bring us, if we overrate the significance of mere outward symbols.

RECOGNITION OF ABILITY

Three boys were trying to make straight lines by walking in the snow. One after another the boys stepped carefully along, placing one foot in front of the other, and trying very hard to make their lines come out straight.

Another boy came along and said with great confidence that he could make a better, straighter line than any of them had done. Challenged, he set out through the snow at great rate. He moved so rapidly, and so unhesitatingly that it didn't seem possible he could succeed.

When they compared his results with the others, however, they had to admit that his line was straighter than any other. Pressed for his secret, he replied, "Do you see that oak tree over there on the hill? I just kept my eyes right on that and walked toward it without paying attention to the snow or to anything around me."

This boy knew in what direction he was going. We can be equally successful in an office career, if our aim is to make the best use of our ability. The greatest satisfaction work can give us, regardless of immediate pay or status, is the opportunity to use and develop our talents.

PRAISE—AND ITS PITFALLS

How can we tell that our ability is recognized, particularly when we do not consider pay as the only criterion? The most widely accepted method is praise. When our boss periodically praises us for our good work, it reassures us that he is pleased with our progress.

Praise, however, has its pitfalls and we should be aware of them so we do not attach undue credence to it.

1. A man may be a fine boss but rarely has a word of praise for his people. He just assumes that they know he appreciates them.

Claire was often left on her own because her boss, the field manager, was away on trips. When he returned, she faithfully recounted all she had accomplished during his absence. He seemed to pay little attention. "As long as things run smoothly, I don't care how you spend your time," he said affably.

Claire was hurt by his apparent indifference. Why, he didn't know whether she took a two-hour lunch hour and went home early, or whether she worked overtime. She wanted some tangible acknowledgment of her conscientiousness.

What Claire did not realize was that her boss was indicating his confidence in her by leaving matters to her discretion.

2. Praise may be omitted due to the press of circumstances.

Mamie found a mistake of $8000 in the advertising budget she was typing. "Would you think my boss would praise me for calling this error to his attention?" was her indignant reaction when he simply rushed away with the papers. Later she learned her boss had been so excited about the mistake that he had entirely forgotten to express his appreciation.

3. Praise may prove embarrassing to the one receiving it.

Pauline had taken home a report and typed it to have it ready for a staff meeting the next morning. The department head noticed the different type face. "Here is a girl," he announced to the other staff members seated around the conference table, "who shows the kind of spirit I like," and then praised her for finishing the report on her own time. It took quite a while before Pauline got back into the good graces of her associates because of the resentment caused by her boss's well-intentioned remarks.

4. Praise may cause a negative reaction.

The office manager assured a clerk who had been in his department over three years, "You're doing all right, Mary. When I hired you, I never thought you'd make it." The girl was more disturbed than pleased. She realized now that all along her boss apparently had had no faith in her. He thought she would fail. After this, she was continually on the lookout for signs of approval from him.

Praise has its place as recognition of our ability. But it does not always evaluate progress. Nor should we place undue reliance on praise. Otherwise we become discouraged when it is withheld. We wonder if we are "slipping" when in reality no slight is intended.

PUBLIC ACKNOWLEDGMENT OF ABILITY

Praise is private and individual. Public acknowledgment of our ability lets the world—even if it is just our little world around us in the office—know what we are doing. It may take many forms, some of them quite subtle:

Claudette was the receptionist in an oculist's office. The doctor for whom she worked gave her some leeway in setting prices. For instance, she might say to a patient:

"Let's see. Suppose we make it twenty dollars for the examination and frame. Ten dollars for the sun glasses. Five dollars for fixing the old frame. That's a total of thirty-five dollars." Claudette got a reputation for "knowing the business." The doctor made it evident that he trusted her good judgment.

Here are some outward forms of recognition of ability which may have come to you:

1. Your name may be listed in the company directory.
2. You may have memo pads with your name printed on them.
3. You may get credit for a suggestion—especially if a suggestion system is in effect.
4. Your boss may ask you to come in and explain to the treasurer some item on the balance sheet you have prepared—rather than go to your office, get the information and then explain it himself.
5. Your boss may dictate, "If you will call my secretary, Miss Knowlton, for an appointment, she will arrange it to our mutual convenience," or, when you have taken a message, "My secretary, Miss Knowlton, has informed me . . ."

6. You may be named to the staff of the house organ or selected as departmental reporter.

7. Your boss may write a letter of commendation to someone higher up, acknowledging your contribution to the success of a goal or project.

8. You may be listed "Registrar" at meetings or put on the committee of arrangements.

9. You may be asked to take a "bow" at an office function in appreciation of your efforts in setting it up.

10. Your boss may instruct you to put your name on a report you have prepared.

11. The preface of a book may contain the inscription: "The author especially extends his thanks to Jessica Smith for typing this manuscript and for her assistance in reading the proof."

Perhaps the greatest recognition of your ability comes to you indirectly through the growing success of the man you work for, particularly if you are a secretary. It is both the penalty and the privilege of those who work in close contact with management that their services often remain anonymous.

ADVANCEMENT

More important than the news, "I've got a raise," is the announcement, "I've been promoted." Many a girl on receiving a new assignment, doesn't ask, nor care, whether the job will carry more pay with it. The chief thing is that she is going up the ladder to success.

Promotions in the office fall into several categories:

1. You are put in a different job classification, such as junior to senior clerk.

2. You become a supervisor, with responsibility for one or more people under you.

3. You are taken out of a group to work for an individual, as a stenographer becoming a secretary.

4. You are transferred from a branch to the home office, or vice versa.

5. An entirely new job is created for you, in which you can utilize some special ability, such as handling all telephone complaints for the department.

6. You are transferred to a job which brings you nearer to attaining your ambitions. This may mean doing creative instead of routine work; using machines that require greater skill; different working hours; more congenial associates.

7. Or, paradoxically, you are so efficient and indispensable, that your boss won't give you up. But in that event, as your boss moves higher up in management, he takes you along so your position involves new duties.

Whatever form your promotion takes, it is deserved recognition for good performance. In a later chapter on "Let Machines Help You Develop," we will point out more specifically the advancement women are making in the business world.

As indicated in the discussion of equal pay, women still face limiting obstacles to advancement. We found that successful women who have been in business over ten years are particularly concerned with top management's attitude toward higher level jobs for women.

Three "career girls," all in their early forties, were talking over their respective job situations. The supervisor for the microfilm and filing records department for a large corporation started the conversation. "They tell us they can't give a woman a job at the policy-making level because she might marry and have a baby. But here are three of us. Even if we did marry, chances are remote that we'd have to give up our career to raise a family!"

The second woman had been told that "she had gone as far as she could" in a multiple-branch bank. She, too, protested against the argument that raising a family was the major deterrent to advancement. "A woman has to stay out only three months or so to have a child, and she can keep in touch with what is going on during that period. Companies send promising young executives away for longer periods to attend executive development programs at colleges. At least, if a married girl is considered for top promotion, they could find out if she plans to continue work, in the event that she has a child. Most women would give an honest answer."

The third member of the group had started some years back as a clerk in the New York sales office of a tobacco company, whose factories and administrative office had been in the south for a number of years. She had worked her way up to head the branch. When the administrative offices were moved to New York, the branch was absorbed. She was made secretary to one of the officers.

When she asked what the future had in store, the explanation was, "We couldn't very well have a woman in the top management of a tobacco company." She is still wondering why not. "It isn't as if women didn't smoke," was the way she looked at it.

These three women were optimistic, however. They felt that as a whole women are making rapid progress in business. And despite the fact that they had personally not attained their highest ambitions, work was a vital part of their lives. All three maintained that they wouldn't give up their job for anything in the world.

ABILITY AND ASSIGNMENTS

Finally, recognition of ability comes from the tone of our relationship with the boss—the way he gives us assignments instead of orders. If he discusses with you what needs to be done, asks for your advice, and leaves it up to you as to how you want to go about the task, you can be assured he regards your ability with the utmost esteem.

CHAPTER V

Loosen the Grip of Tension

Two girls were waiting for a third to join them for lunch. She rushed in breathlessly.

"Sorry to be late," she apologized, "but our place was all in a dither. Last night we had a long draft of a report Mr. Swift has to give before the bar association. He wanted to take twenty-five copies along on the two o'clock plane. I stayed late to type it, and he took the copy home to be edited. This morning, another lawyer dropped in and suggested some last-minute changes. I couldn't start on the stencils till ten o'clock. In two places he had left blanks, for copies of resolutions to be filled in.

"His secretary instructed me to leave a couple of inches of space for the resolutions. When she finally came in with them, around quarter to twelve, I couldn't fit them in the space I left. That meant doing two stencils over. Right now the report is in the mimeograph department. I only hope nothing more goes wrong!"

This is a typical case of how tension builds up in an office. Everyone excited about getting the job done! Things going wrong at the last minute! But it usually comes out all right in the end.

Such incidents are a normal part of office life. We learn to take them in stride. And we react to them in a normal way.

Tension in the human body is like steam in the locomotive.

When we sleep, tension is usually lowest. When we start to work, it rises. After the day's demands are over, we let our tensional level fall, just as the pressure of steam in the engine is allowed to drop.

Tension, or emotional energy, should not be throttled, according to Dr. Frederick W. Dershimer, Director of Psychiatry, Du Pont Company, whose work is described by Howard Whitman in "Emotional Upsets Are Good for You," in *Collier's*.

To help explain his ideas, he built a gadget showing man as a steam engine. A valve at the neck allowed emotional energy generated in the boiler of the viscera to pass freely up to the brain and operate the engine.

Normally, this steam engine operates on whatever pressure is needed to do the job at hand. Suppose you are driving in the country. Your emotional engine is running on four or five pounds of steam because that's all you need to operate the brain for such an easy, routine activity.

Suddenly a car comes veering at you from the opposite lane of the road. Emotions of fear, shock, alarm shoot the steam pressure in your emotional boiler up to fourteen or twenty pounds. That is nature working on your side, protecting you. You're going to need the additional energy. If the valve is open, that energy goes right to the engine, sends the brain speeding up to its full potential. Result: your brain works with fantastic speed and effectiveness. You act quickly and avoid an accident.

Only when the valve is open can man's basic force—emotional energy—surge freely to the brain and give it the power to think swiftly and effectively. From this power of free-flowing emotional energy come the inventions of man, his courage, his imagination, his industry, his accomplishment.

Dr. Dershimer adds, "Trying to control our inner reactions is detrimental to our efficiency and dangerous to our mental health. We must, of course, control our outward behavior to get along in the world."

CONTINUOUS TENSION

When tension persists over protracted periods, pressure keeps accumulating instead of periodically dropping back to normal. It's still there when we begin work again in the morning. No engine could stand the strain of being continually steamed up. Build pressure sufficiently high and it will "blow its top." People act the same way.

HOW CAN YOU TELL WHEN YOU'RE TENSE?

When you ride in a train, every so often you see a row of chains or ropes hanging from a bar placed above and across the railroad tracks. This is a "tell-tale"—a danger signal—warning freight crewmen of an overhead tunnel or bridge.

Tension, too, has signals to warn us that there's danger ahead—that we are reaching a boiling point. Some of the more obvious "tell-tales" are:

1. You can't sleep well, are unable to relax, are restless, on edge, depressed.

2. You are tired out at the end of the day. Judith Chase Churchill in an article, *To Do More Work with Less Fatigue,* says that "Unnecessary pressure and high pace tenses and exhausts you and decreases efficiency."[1]

We have already seen how emotional energy rises at times when it is necessary to "get up steam," when driving a car. Some people, however, don't drive along at an easy, relaxed pace. On the contrary, they imagine that the more they keep their eyes and all bodily muscles intent, the more quickly they can react when danger arises. But experiments show they react more quickly from a relaxed than from a tense condition. If you are all keyed up in expectation of danger, then, when the danger suddenly confronts you, you must

---

[1] Judith Chase Churchill. "To Do More Work with Less Fatigue." *Woman's Home Companion,* November, 1952.

first relax before you can re-direct your muscles in the proper direction. In other words, you must first let your emotional energy get through to your brain.

Thus, if you do your work in a relaxed, even-paced manner, you use less energy, are less fatigued and accomplish the most.

3. Your physical mannerisms betray tension. An executive says, "My secretary has completely ruined my nerves by tearing waste paper into tiny shreds, over and over, before throwing it into the basket." Dr. Edmund Jacobson in a chapter on "Tense Persons" in his book, *You Must Relax* describes a stenographer who visited him: "This young lady of twenty-five shows signs which will not be hard to read. If you watch her at work, you note that she holds her back and neck somewhat stiffly. At times she almost wriggles as if to get herself in a more comfortable position, while she frowns, wrinkles her forehead or sighs as if worried or distressed. She scarcely sits still for as long as a minute, always finding occasion to move some part, such as a hand or leg. You do not feel at rest while speaking with her."[1]

Other indications of tension are twitching your mouth, grimacing or fussing with your head and face in a variety of jerky motions. You may tap your fingers, fiddle with small objects, bite your finger nails. Or you may push up your hair from your forehead in repetitive gestures. A photograph in *Life* magazine is descriptive in its caption: "Tension shows in twisted hands and peeled nail polish."

4. You speak somewhat fast and a little too much. Your voice becomes strident, high-pitched. If talking in a shrill voice becomes a habit it will be a detriment to your advancement. Miss Beatrice Desfosses, speech consultant for the Berkeley Schools in New York and vicinity, in a survey of 1000 business leaders in the metropolitan area, was told by a

[1] Edmund Jacobson, M.D. *You Must Relax*, 3rd ed. New York: Mc-Graw-Hill Book Company, 1948.

top flight executive with an air of finality that he would not hire a girl with a shrill voice, no matter how good her skills. If you make an effort to speak slowly, in a well-pitched tone, on the other hand, you'll find your tension reduced.

5. You stick grimly to a task—regardless of whether it must be completed or not. Try to cut the rope of tension that ties you to your work by alternating between two or three jobs whenever possible in any given stretch. Even if a job must be finished in a stated time, take a brief respite before the final spurt.

6. You become impatient, are easily upset, burst out in temper at the slightest provocation. This puts others on their guard against you. In turn, you become even more tense—provoking the very type of situation which sets you off anew.

7. You have "misunderstandings." Dr. Verne Kallejian, psychologist at the Institute of Industrial Relations, University of California, found that one factor which interferes with the development of understanding is that when people are tense they tend to be less alert to what is happening around them.

8. You make mistakes. In bookkeeping, you transpose figures, like "589" for "598." In typing, you reverse letters, like "het" for "the." Stenographers report that often when they are asked to do a letter over, they repeat the very mistake they are trying to correct. That's because their mind is so blocked up with tension that they can't think straight.

"Try to avoid getting Mr. Bronwell for dictation," a girl in a stenography pool told a newcomer. "He always finds something wrong." When the newcomer was assigned to Mr. Bronwell for some letters, she determined that he would find her work perfect. But she was so nervous in her desire to be accurate that she made several foolish errors.

9. You are always on the verge of quitting (at least in your own mind). This undermines your morale because you justify

indifference and poor quality workmanship with the attitude, "Why bother? I'm going to leave anyhow." Thus, you never derive the satisfaction that comes from throwing yourself wholeheartedly into a task.

CAUSES OF TENSION

Whenever danger signals appear, we look deep for the "why" behind them. Before we know how to act, we must know the causes that create our problem.

Tension is caused:

1. When people are improperly selected in the first place. The boss or personnel executive may unintentionally make choices which later lead to tension, or they may have no alternative. The person selected is seldom responsible for the fact that she may unwittingly cause friction. But she should be sure that she does not add fuel to the flame by her actions or her conduct.

2. When situations develop during the course of office relationships which touch off temperamental fuses. Presumably, if it is within our power to change such situations and alleviate tension, we will do so. On the other hand, some people thrive on tension. They could accomplish their work much faster if they did not spend so much time telling everyone how busy they are. It builds their ego to be rushed. If they are forced to cancel appointments, they feel it proves to their friends and associates that they are indispensable in their jobs.

SELECTION

Tension situations which arise out of improper selection may be grouped in the following broad categories:

1. An executive may have a preconceived idea of the type of girl he wants, without considering her qualifications for the work. He may hire someone simply because she unconsciously reminds him of his mother or a former sweetheart.

Employment agencies claim that executives on occasion give them detailed specifications down to physical characteristics. One man wants "a lively brunette type." Another is convinced that "a girl of German parentage is bound to be efficient."

An article in the *Saturday Evening Post* tells how Katharine Gibbs sent two of its best students to be interviewed by the sales manager of a New York tea company. "Both were rejected without explanation. Two other sets of girls were similarly rebuffed before the personnel manager confided sheepishly that he couldn't stand turban-type hats. Such cases are not unusual. A rubber company executive refuses to hire girls under five feet, eight inches tall. A newspaper representative insists on redheads."

Unrealistic selection of employees may lead to tension because others wonder on what basis a candidate was chosen. But good performance, even if the initial selection was not well made, will do much to convince her associates that a girl is rightfully entitled to the job she is holding.

2. People of different levels of educational background may be teamed up.

A research laboratory in rural 'Pennsylvania was staffed almost exclusively by scientists, most of them college men. They were serviced by a pool of stenographers. Obviously, the enterprising girls in the vicinity migrated to the cities which offered more opportunity. The laboratory had to recruit from the less ambitious who stayed at home—usually with the intention of marrying as soon as possible.

The men.were handicapped by the mediocre ability of the stenographers. The girls had difficulty with the technical dictation. The laboratory became an "armed camp" before the situation was rectified by a training program to upgrade the girls' skills.

3. People may be arbitrarily thrown together. An example

is a government office, where the stenographers and clerks under Civil Service must be picked from a list that is submitted to their superior.

A Washington attorney, head of a Bureau, found this practice particularly trying when girls on the lists submitted to him had the backing of their Congressmen. "They are the daughters of some local 'big shot' back home." He admitted that he might unjustifiably be disposed against a girl, just because he might be under some compulsion to accept her. "It's surprising, though," he concluded optimistically, "how soon this prejudice vanishes if the girl has an agreeable personality, and fills the job on her own merits."

4. A girl may not be congenial to the rest of the group.

Laurel, a newcomer to the advertising department, belonged to a strict religious sect. She took part in a number of church activities. She did not drink or smoke.

The other girls were not so strait-laced. Some would take a cocktail at a Christmas or birthday party. Those who did not drink nevertheless joined the fun over a glass of ginger ale. Laurel openly declared such conduct hypocrisy. The girls respected her for sticking to her standards, but they were ill-at-ease and wary in her presence.

The value of selecting compatible groups for the office is recognized by employers. Helen Edwards, owner of "Helen Edwards and Staff" in Los Angeles, who specializes in matching personalities of employers and job seekers, claims that business men today call up and say: "We want you to send over one or two applicants for an opening in our —— department. You know the type you've sent before. We must have someone who will fit in with our staff and surroundings!"

5. An employee may be over-qualified.

You've heard of children with a high I.Q. who are brighter than their classmates, yet have poor marks. Bored with the too simple assignments of their class, they have paid no attention to their studies. Placed in groups with exceptional children, or promoted to a higher grade, they do well.

When an over-qualified girl finds herself in a mediocre job, she likewise may turn in a poorer performance than a person with less intelligence and ability. The work has no challenge and her energy is directed to brooding about the fact that the job is beneath her.

She is likely to snap at her associates and accept assignments from her boss grudgingly because she is continuously on the defensive.

The message of this book, "You can make your own job, if you work in an office," is directed specifically to anyone caught in such a position.

TENSE RELATIONSHIPS

Tension situations which arise out of office relationships may be classified as follows:

1. Promotions may cause tensions all along the line. The person who is promoted is usually glad of the advancement but may become worried because of the new responsibilities. The security of the person above the one promoted may be threatened because she fears a possible competitor.

The problem often resolves itself when the girl who has been promoted becomes familiar with her new duties, and when she shows by her attitude that she is fair and square and does not try to dislodge others.

2. A superior may carry over an unfortunate past experience into the present situation.

John Claxton, a young executive with a master's degree in business administration, came to a company where most of the employees worked at their own pace. Since he was high-powered and efficient, he always kept after everyone to check that his assignments would be finished on time.

Then he hired Doris, who was capable and conscientious. From force of habit, Claxton continued putting deadlines on his assignments to Doris. This resulted in more pressure than previously, since she was now the only one doing his work, which formerly had been divided among different stenographers and typists.

Eventually, Claxton noticed that Doris always made it a point to have the work ready promptly. He realized that there was no need to push her. Her patience won over his skepticism. Now he says, "I don't have to tell you when I'm in a hurry— you seem to have things finished even before I give them to you."

3. Administrative changes at higher levels may affect employees down the line.

An executive may "inherit" a girl who has worked for his predecessor. She may feel she knows more about the details of the job than he does. He may actually be dependent on her yet resent her "power" over him.

In public offices, political changes may inject tensions.

For more than twenty years, Irene MacIntosh had been borough clerk of Ridgefield Center. No discount passed her unnoticed. No scrap of paper was wasted. The councilmen, who year in and year out were of the same political faith, left the management of the office in her hands.

Then a member of the opposition party was elected to the council. Long in the minority group, he now took advantage of his new position to show the voters he could "clean house." Every day Irene received instructions from him about the most minor details. He asked for an accounting of every penny, peered into every file. The other councilmen, who trusted Irene implicitly, were stymied. They couldn't ask him to leave Irene alone, because he would have suspected that they were trying to cover up or hide extravagances.

Irene was smart enough to realize that it wasn't her work

which was under scrutiny. She made every effort to accommodate the new councilman with information. This flattered him into thinking he had the inside track on affairs.

4. Physical environment may be responsible for tension. A classic example is the open-versus-closed window controversy, fortunately disappearing with air conditioning.

In a mail order house a bookkeeper, Vera, had her desk alongside an aisle. At first she didn't mind when people stopped to say a friendly good morning or good night. But she soon was entrusted with a message for everyone in the vicinity. A score of times a day she was interrupted with, "Have you seen Mr. Jones—[or Mr. Smith, or whomever they were seeking]— pass by?" Apparently she was supposed to notice everyone who conceivably passed her desk. Other times it was, "When you see Mr. Jones, will you tell him I'm looking for him?"

"I felt I would scream at the next person who stopped to speak to me," she told us.

A slight change in layout, to which her boss readily acquiesced, spared her nerves.

Noise is notorious as a source of tension. Managements try to keep it at a minimum by insulation and partitions. Employees can do their part by being considerate.

Also, we can train ourselves to hear only those things we want to hear. An interesting comment in this connection was made by a married woman who returned to a business office.

She said, "The first thing I had to do when I took this job was to adjust to noise. At home, I always had my ear cocked to noises inside and outside the house. I could tell whether the children were safe by the kind of noises they made. Here, in the office, I have to shut out noise. If I were aware of all the telephone conversations, office machines, and miscellaneous sounds, I'd never be able to concentrate on what I'm doing."

5. Personal affairs may become involved in the job.

When Theresa was hired to work for the president of a mid-western company, a condition of employment was that her hours would be irregular. The president maintained two offices—one in Chicago and one in his factory in an Illinois city. She never knew in advance when he would turn up after a visit to his Chicago office—often at quarter to five. During the day she would have relatively little to do, but as soon as he arrived it meant rushing till about seven. As long as she was single, she simply telephoned her mother to keep dinner warm. On the way home, she could look forward to relaxation after a hectic day.

When Theresa married, her husband, who called for her in the car, was often kept waiting. He would read the evening paper from beginning to end with increasing irritation—hungry for the dinner which would not be on the table until after eight o'clock. Theresa, high-strung after working under pressure, wouldn't be able to eat at all when supper finally was ready.

This girl decided her marriage was more important than her career. She found a job with less money, but with nine-to-five hours.

SUMMARY

A certain amount of pressure is part of living and stimulates us to action. Only 9 per cent of girls interviewed in a survey mentioned being unhappy about pressure.

Too long sustained and too continuous pressure results in undesirable tension. Some elements in a tension-producing situation are beyond our control. But we can reduce friction if we recognize the symptoms of tension, analyze the causes, and act in good faith.

CHAPTER VI

Test Yourself for Tact

TACT is a quick or intuitive appreciation of what is proper or right. It can be described as "social consciousness." A person knows how she herself thinks or feels when she acts in a particular manner. Therefore, when another human being acts in a similar way, she believes that the other person must be experiencing similar reactions to those which she had when she was behaving in a like manner. This indirect consciousness of the thoughts and feelings of others is the basis of tact.

Tact is the most important quality for success as a secretary, according to the combined opinion of the "Seraphic Secretaries of America," a group limited to one hundred secretaries of famous men.

A tactful person has four attributes:

1. She is sensitive about the feelings of others.

Annette Deming was a schoolteacher. For one month each summer she substituted for the administrative assistant at a personnel consulting service.

"Miss Deming tells everyone to ask for her by name," said the administrative assistant, provoked. "Everybody wants to talk to her personally. She gives them the impression that she is in charge here. Each year it takes me several months, after she's been in the office, to re-establish my identity."

As a teacher, Miss Deming is in the habit of announcing her name with authority. She transfers this trait automatically when she works in an office. But she lacks tact because she doesn't perceive the effect this has on the clients of the consulting service. Nor does she realize that the administrative assistant is sensitive about her status.

2. She is aware of the consequences of her conduct.

Louise asked for some extra time off at lunch. When she returned at two o'clock, her hair was set in curls which had not been combed out.

"I granted her the longer lunch hour without asking the reason," her chief admitted, "but it was tactless to leave her hair in such a fashion that everyone could tell right off that she had been to the beauty parlor. Now the others will want the same privilege."

3. She reasons with subtle discernment.

Vera was a free-lancer for an employment agency that specialized in temporary jobs. On Friday evening, as she completed her week in a stock broker's office, the man for whom she was working gave her a batch of mail to seal. Included was a questionnaire from the agency, asking whether the person sent him was satisfactory. She noticed that he had filled in, "Very capable, willing and conscientious."

When Vera reported at the agency on Monday for a new assignment, the personnel interviewer said, "The stock broker was very complimentary about your work," and read her the comments. Vera acted pleasantly surprised, although she knew what was coming. "I didn't want to take away her pleasure at telling me good news."

Another aspect of subtle reasoning is illustrated by an incident which, in some form or other, happens to all of us:

The plant superintendent had asked Dorothy for some specifications. She spent quite a time hunting for them in the file, in her desk, all over the office. Her boss insisted she had them.

Finally, when he was out of his private office, she found them in his desk. When he returned, he was accompanied by another executive. "I knew you'd find them," he smiled when she handed him the specifications. Her impulse was to let him know that he, not she, had put away this material.

Instead, she quietly went back to her desk, but could not help overhearing her boss say, "She's a wonderful girl. . . . Nothing she can't put her finger on, no matter how forgetful I am."

4. She has insight into the motives of others.

Mr. Hayward, an architect, left Hilda, his capable secretary, in charge while he went away on his vacation. He knew that some technical questions would arise which might require decisions that Hilda could not make. He therefore entrusted these to Don Ricker, one of the younger architects. He also asked Don to give Hilda advice on any technical correspondence should she need it.

The first day Mr. Hayward was away, Don came into Hilda's office right after nine o'clock and demanded to see the mail. Then he dictated replies, most of them to the effect that "your letter has been received in Mr. Hayward's absence. It will have his attention on his return."

Hilda was furious. She was able to write such letters herself! But she tactfully refrained from commenting. She realized that this was Don's first chance to "show off."

Her judgment was correct. After a few days he left her alone, and there were no hard feelings between them.

TECHNIQUES OF TACT

Thousands of examples exist in our day-to-day life in the office that can teach us how to be tactful.

1. If we can't understand why we've antagonized someone, we can reverse the role. Stop to think how you would feel under similar circumstances. When you discern the reason why the other person was offended, it impresses itself on your mind. You probably won't repeat the same mistake.

2. If we sense someone is pleased with one of our comments, actions or courtesies, analyze what prompted the pleasant reaction. Remember to do or say the same thing on future occasions.

3. If a tactless remark disturbs us, let's try to see ourselves as others see us. Maybe we can discover what aroused the other person or provoked her tactlessness—and benefit by this discovery.

4. Thank others if they are tactful to us. The other person will be pleased by your thoughtfulness. You will form the habit of courtesy, and as a result will spontaneously respond in like fashion till it becomes second nature to you to be courteous.

5. Listen with "a third ear" for overtones of tact in conversations that go on in our presence. You will develop a fine sensitivity and perception of the techniques of tact.

Start by testing yourself for tact in the following cases all taken from actual occurrences. We tried out these questions on a cross-section of executives, on girls in all types of office jobs and on the general public. They did not always agree on the best course of action. Rather, they felt that the most tactful conduct in each situation depended on variable considerations.

What would you do in each of the following instances?

1. It is the custom in a company for executives to sign a slip acknowledging new inserts for an insurance manual. The industrial relations manager, comes into the office of the

clerk in charge of distributing the inserts. He is accompanied by the president.

"I never received my March 7 revision," he accuses the girl. When she goes for another copy, she notices he has signed the acknowledgment card for the March 7 insert. Should she:

A. Show him his signature, to prove both to him and to the president that she has not been remiss?

B. Say, "I'm sorry that you were overlooked?"

C. Tell him, "I'll check up to see what happened?"

She is undoubtedly burning with a desire to redeem herself both in front of the president and the industrial relations manager. But it's never good policy to show up anyone. She need not take the blame to the extent of saying "I'm sorry you were overlooked," which implies there has been an oversight. But the middle-of-the-road statement, to the effect that she will see what happened, is both tactful and truthful.

2. A girl in a payroll department takes down time-card corrections as they are called in over the telephone. The other girls know that she continuously receives personal calls from her boy friend on this wire. The rule is no personal calls except during lunch hour. Should they:

A. Report the girl to the supervisor?

B. Ignore the matter and hope the supervisor will find out about it?

C. Have several of the girls in the group talk to the offender and show her the unfairness of taking advantage?

The desire to report the girl might be prompted by jealousy that she has such an attentive boy friend and also by the fact that she has a telephone at her disposal. Much depends in this situation on whether the other girls are inconvenienced by these telephone calls. Does her talking disturb them in their work? Or are they forced to work longer or harder to make up for the time lost by the girl while phoning? If such is the case, they can appeal to her fairness. But chances are that such an approach will set the girl against them and disrupt office harmony. It probably is best to wait until the supervisor catches on.

3. You have typed a memo dictated by the office manager to be signed by the vice president. You are to bring it to the vice president's office, and his secretary is to send it out. The vice president makes some changes, asks you to retype the memo and bring it back right away. Should you:

A. Retype the memo and return it to the vice president without mentioning the changes to your boss?

B. Retype it, return it to the vice president and tell your boss about the changes afterward?

C. Show the edited memo to your boss so he can discuss the changes with the vice president if he wants to?

Here are some points you will have to consider in this case. How close is your boss's desk—right in the same room with yours? Then you can make it apparent to him what you are doing. But if he is some distance away, and perhaps can't be located immediately, then the best thing to do is to bring the typed memo back to the vice president, but hunt up your boss right away to show him the corrected copy. You owe loyalty to the man who is your immediate supervisor. Unless—and this is unlikely—the vice president has asked you to keep the revision confidential, he will only respect you for your alertness in keeping your own boss so promptly informed, in the event your boss should discuss the changes with him.

4. You are substituting for another girl during vacation. Her desk is ink-stained and sloppy. Letterheads are dog-eared and yellowed from exposure. Should you:

A. Work at the disorderly desk, but get a small supply of clean stationery for your temporary use?

B. Clean the desk, and supply it with fresh stationery, sharpened pencils, new blotter?

Your first impulse will be to clean the desk. Not only do you like to work at a clean place, but you don't want others to think you aren't tidy. And the sloppy desk will reflect on you while you are temporarily using it.

But hold on! Don't do too thorough a job. Get clean paper for your use, but leave the old paper underneath. Dust the desk, but don't do a spring housecleaning job on the ink spots. The girl who is on vacation doesn't want to return to find her bad habits the subject of widespread attention.

5. Your boss, Mr. Durance, is on the telephone. Another executive comes into the office and asks you, "Who's Mr. Durance talking to?" Should you:

A. Say, "I'm sorry I don't know," even if you do know?
B. Tell him whom your boss is talking to?
C. Intimate that you don't think you have a right to give him this information?

Probably A. After all, you *don't* know who your boss is talking to. Suppose Mr. Durance has asked for Mr. Thompson, the executive vice president. But instead of Mr. Thompson, he gets Tyler, Thompson's assistant, who happens to be a close friend of your boss. The visiting executive overhears Durance making an appointment with Tyler to play golf. He jumps to the erroneous conclusion that Durance is playing golf with the executive vice president, since you informed him that that was whom your boss was talking to. This misunderstanding can cause some hard feelings. And all the while you thought you had told the truth!

6. While your boss is away, one of the men in the company comes to your office. "I've been elected secretary of the Cost Control Association. Mr. Miller, [your boss] suggested that you would do some clerical work for me in connection with this association. I've got some notices that must be in the mail tonight." You happen to be busy with some first-of-the-month statements. Should you:

A. Tell this man your boss hasn't informed you that you are to do this work?

B. Do his work, at the expense of delaying your statements?

C. Tell him you are busy with your statements?

You may want to refuse the job because you resent the intrusion and the way you are approached, when you haven't consented to accept this added work. But first inquire how much work is involved. If it takes only a few minutes, perhaps you can crowd it in. If it is really too time-consuming, explain your predicament. But offer to do as many notices as you can, and suggest some others in the office who might "pitch in." You owe it to your boss to be as cooperative in his absence, as if he were in the office.

7. Beth is the Girl Friday in the publicity department. She always rushes into the mimeograph department at 4:30 P.M. with a batch of releases that must go out that day. The mimeographers are forced to stay overtime, usually without advance notice. Beth knows she causes this inconvenience, for which she is partly personally responsible, because in some instances she could get some of the work over to them earlier. But she shrugs off any discussion. "How would you like to have my job," she snaps back, "I'm often here till seven o'clock. I expect a little help." You are the supervisor of the mimeograph department. Should you:

A. Contact the publicity director and report Beth's attitude?

B. Tell the girls in the department they have to accept the unscheduled overtime?

C. Go to your own supervisor about this problem?

You can go to your supervisor for the sake of being on record but you cannot expect him or her to solve your problem. Therefore, this line of action gains you nothing. To contact the publicity director would antagonize Beth so that you would get even less cooperation from her. Temporarily, the girls will have to accept the overtime. But you can try to plan your work so that you can put everyone on the releases in case they arrive late. And when Beth sees your good intentions, she may reverse her attitude and be willing to meet you half way.

8. One of your associates confides in you that she is taking the day off to help her uncle, a florist, who has an order to decorate for a large wedding. She has told her supervisor that she has to go to the hospital for a check-up.

On the day she is out, a serious question arises in connection with her work. The supervisor doesn't know where to reach her. Should you:

A. Act as if the situation doesn't concern you?
B. Give the supervisor the florist's number, trusting to luck that the deception won't be discovered?
C. Telephone the girl yourself, and find out what she wants to do?

Much depends on the type of girl. If she is your friend, as is implied by the fact that she confided in you, naturally you'll call her yourself. If she is a snippy type, who told you about working for her uncle just to let you know that she "gets away with things," then it would be advisable to act as if the situation isn't any of your business. The difficulty with this decision is that your own conscience will trouble you. So you might telephone her, but be prepared to be snubbed. She may not thank you for "butting in."

9. You are a department clerk in a college. You work for several professors. You also have administrative duties on which you report directly to the registrar in the administrative office.

The registrar appreciates your cooperative attitude, and you get along well with her. One of your professors has a run-in with the registrar. He insists that he has sent in his grades. She cannot locate them. He asks you to go to the administrative office and search through the folders for his sheet of grades, to prove he is right. Should you:

A. Follow his instructions and antagonize the registrar?

B. Tell him that his instructions are contrary to the policy of the administrative office?

C. Talk over your problems with the registrar and solicit her help in finding the sheet?

The answer is C—with these reservations. Don't cast aspersions on the professor. Rather, exonerate his behavior with "professors have so much on their minds at examination time." And don't antagonize the registrar by implying that you *know* she has the grade sheet. Just treat the whole incident as casual checking.

10. Mr. Cline, a personnel consultant, telephones a labor union office for a copy of the labor agreement with the Ace Machine Tool Company which has retained him. The contract does not arrive for two days. The consultant asks the telephone operator to check up. Should she say:

A. "Did you forget to send the contract about which Mr. Cline telephoned you two days ago?"

B. "Mr. Cline asked me to call you for a copy of the labor agreement with the Ace Machine Tool Company," (even though she knows he has already telephoned).

Always give the other person the benefit of the doubt. In this instance, politely request a copy of the contract. If one has already gone forward, they'll tell you soon enough.

11. One of the department heads reporting to your boss has acquired a reputation for "making a play" for some of the girls who work under him. The girls hint to you they don't want to complain, for fear he will hold it against them. One girl has left the department at her husband's insistence, but, of course, this reason was not given in her exit interview at the employment office. Should you:

A. Inform your boss about this situation?

B. Take the attitude that it does not concern you?

C. Talk informally with the department head yourself, trying to get over to him how the girls feel?

The answer to this problem depends on several factors. You'd have to be certain that these alleged "attentions" are not exaggerated rumors spread by a few girls. There are some sirens or *femmes fatales* in every department who misconstrue courtesies. Are these attentions "little indecencies?" Or do they fall in the category of giving a girl a lift, or good-humored "kidding"? Even the girl who resigned may have been trying to get her husband jealous. Generally speaking, it's best to ignore the gossip. If, however, you are an older woman, and the department head is a young man, you can safely have a sincere talk with him. If you are a young girl, and he is of the same age or older, on the other hand, he could construe such a talk as an overture on your part to attract his attention to yourself.

12. Your boss is chairman of a business conference. A few weeks before the meeting date, the chief speaker writes that he cannot appear. You relay this message to your boss, who is away at a branch office. He wires you to contact Mr. Young as a replacement. Should you:

A. Tell Mr. Young that the other speaker has cancelled his appearance and that is why you are calling him at a relatively late date to substitute?

B. Pretend the program is just being set up?

Invite the man, without apologies. He probably surmises what has happened, anyway. But it's not likely that he will ask you outright whether he is second choice, particularly if he wants to accept and is pleased to have this opportunity of participating in the conference.

13. Your boss continually keeps papers that belong in the centralized file. The file supervisor accuses you of not getting these folders back to her. Should you:

A. Tell your boss about your predicament?

B. Take the folders away surreptitiously when he is not around?

C. Suggest to the file supervisor that she talk to him herself?

Are you going to admit to the file supervisor that you haven't enough courage to talk to your boss yourself? Of course not! You needn't tell him, in so many words, that the file supervisor is disturbed about his tactics, because that would put him in the wrong. Rather, whenever you are working with him and have an opportunity, pick up a folder from his desk and ask courteously, "I wonder whether you're through with this? The file room likes to get the folders back as soon as possible."

14. You are keeping a personal appointment in another section of the city at noon. Should you:

A. Hope you will get back in time, and leave the office without comment?

B. Tell your employer that although you will do your best to be back on time, you may be unavoidably detained?

C. Talk to your employer in advance of making the appointment, so he can let you know if it interferes with his plans?

If at all possible, check with your employer before making plans. But if he is not available, or you don't want to disturb him, choose B. If you must leave without telling him, either write a note or telephone if you are delayed.

15. You frequently share-ride with a man in an adjacent office. One day several girls come to your office and start laughing a little too loudly. The man happens to be dictating and shuts the door between the two offices in a rather pointed manner. You feel embarrassed and annoyed. Should you:

A. Go home with some one else that evening?

B. Pretend you are working overtime and aren't ready when he leaves?

C. Ride with him, and apologize for the noise which you realize must have disturbed him?

By all means ride with him. Otherwise you might as well have the bricklayers seal up that door between your offices, because of the enmity and hard feelings that will result. Remember, the man by this time is probably a little shamefaced about his impulsive action. If you offer to take the blame, chances are good he will minimize the importance of the situation. "I shouldn't have been so hasty either," will probably be his mollified answer.

16. An executive said to the receptionist: "Will you get Mr. Walstrom on the telephone? I think his number is Woodridge 7-2800. Without contradicting him, she dialed Woodridge 2-7800, the correct number. When she handed him the phone, the executive smiled, "I always have a good memory for numbers." Should she:

A. Correct him, so he will not call the wrong number in the future?

B. Pay no attention to his comment?

C. Say, "I'll always be glad to check any numbers for you?"

Your first impulse should always be to "save face." Either ignoring the comment with a smile or making a remark such as indicated in C is appropriate.

17. An advance draft of an organizational policy change is on your desk. Your chief has instructed you to keep this confidential. One of the department heads looks over your shoulder as you are checking the draft, and reads it. He is quite disturbed by the contents, which will affect him. Should you:

A. Ask him not to mention to your boss that he saw the memo on your desk?

B. Trust to luck that he won't mention it before it is issued?

C. Tell your boss about the incident, which implicates both

you, for leaving the memo exposed, and the man, for reading it.

Trust the department head to be ethical enough to make no mention of the incident, but watch out in the future when he comes into your office if you are working on confidential matters. If, however, he mentions the information, face up to what has happened. Otherwise, your boss may worry about the leak in his organization, or he may accuse the wrong people of divulging information in advance.

18. Today is your birthday. A "special" young man is taking you to lunch. Just before noon, the president's secretary calls you in to take dictation from the president, because she is busy with something else. You are anxious to make a good impression. This could mean a job in the private office for you. Should you:

A. Disappoint the young man, or let him wait all lunch hour, since you can't telephone him before you go in to take dictation as he obviously has already left his office?

B. Tell the president that you have a luncheon date?

C. Confide in the president's secretary?

Enlist the help of the president's secretary. She's a woman, too, and women love to conspire where men are concerned. Tell her where the young man will be waiting. Perhaps she can get word to him through the switchboard operator. Or, she may be able to maneuver things around tactfully so you won't have to stay in the president's office long. She'll also contrive to give you a "high sign" while you are taking dictation to assure you, if possible, that she has successfully contacted your friend.

19. While your boss is out of town, one of the company's best customers comes to call to take him to lunch. Disappointed, he invites you to lunch instead. You know this man is married. Should you:

A. Accept the invitation?

B. Tell him your boss doesn't approve of your going out with customers?

C. Thank him, but say you have another luncheon engagement which you can't very well break?

A somewhat similar question was asked in a test given by the National Secretaries Association. This group voted C the most tactful solution.

20. You telephone a trade associaton for some information appearing in one of their bulletins. The librarian offers to call you back as soon as she locates the material. In the interim, you find the bulletin. The information you want means taking down two or three pages in shorthand. When she phones back, should you:

A. Let her know you have found the bulletin and save her the time of reading the excerpt?

B. Pretend to take down what she reads you and thank her for all her trouble?

If you told her you had found the bulletin, little time would be saved at best. It's worth sacrificing these few moments for tact. So by all means let her read the data and put her in the position of doing you a favor.

21. You are a dental assistant. A patient has started reading a story in the current issue of an expensive fiction magazine while waiting for her appointment. When she leaves, she asks you whether she can take the magazine along to finish her story. You know she is well able to afford to buy a copy—which is available on the newsstands. Should you:

A. Let her take the magazine and ask her to bring it back?

B. Tell her the magazines are for all patients and you are not permitted to let any be taken away?

C. Say, "Is it the current issue?" and hope she will take the hint?

If you can put a polite enough inflection in your voice, C should be sufficient to make her realize your embarrassment.

22. You are employed by Mr. Lightner, one of the attorneys in a firm of several law partners. Since you also do work for the other lawyers, you have a key to all the private offices. The prosecutor, who is a close friend of your boss, comes in one afternoon, while your boss is detained in court. The prosecutor tells you he will wait for Mr. Lightner, because an urgent situation has arisen, and then asks, "Is there a couch somewhere around here? I'm completely exhausted. I just left the hospital on Monday." Your office has no facilities. One of the other partners, however, has a settee in his office. Should you:

A. Open the door of that office with your pass key, checking first that the desk is locked and no papers around?
B. Tell the prosecutor no couch is available?
C. Explain to the prosecutor that one of the partners has a settee (mentioning the person's name) but you don't know whether he would want you to open his door.

The answer to this question almost completely hinges on personalities and relationships. If the partner in whose office the settee is located and the prosecutor are not on amicable terms, then the prosecutor will be quick enough to tell you, "Don't bother." If you know that it would benefit the partner to get closer to the prosecutor, you might open the door, first checking that no papers are on the desk.

You'll have to consider the type of man the partner is. A stickler for conventions? A friendly extrovert who likes to do favors?

You probably won't have exactly the same problem, but similar ones occur where you, or someone else, wants to use a phone in a private office, where you need to borrow equipment without checking, or where there is occasion to invade privacy.

23. You have a message for your boss who is in conference. Should you:

A. Break into his office and give him the message?

B. Motion him to the door?

C. Write the message on a slip of paper and quietly hand it to your boss?

Hand him the message on a slip of paper. This does not interrupt the meeting. It does not commit him to an answer— as is the case when you telephone him. And, if your boss makes some verbal comment while he reads the message, or issues instructions in reply to the note, be cautious about your own comments in answering him.

CHAPTER VII

Cooperation Cuts Corners

Madeline was a staff assistant in a personnel office. She had worked her way up from a clerk. All the other young women in the group were college graduates. Madeline was on the defensive with these girls, who had achieved comparable positions in much less time. She was reluctant to explain company policies and procedures to new members of the staff. "Let them learn the hard way, as I did," was her attitude.

One day the department head was taken ill. Madeline was chosen to take charge of the group's activities, because she was still the best equipped person to step in, although the others had special skills which she had not mastered. To make a success of her temporary appointment, she needed their advice and the benefit of their knowledge.

In spite of the fact that she had treated the others in such a hostile manner, they realized her predicament and came forward with offers of assistance. But Madeline let her long-smoldering feeling of inferiority get the upper hand. She openly taunted the others that college education doesn't get you anywhere—the company had to take someone with practical experience when they were in a pinch.

Naturally, that ended the attempts of the other girls to help her. When the department head returned, Madeline was asked to resign because of the antagonism that had developed.

CO-WORKER COOPERATION

Madeline did not understand the principles of cooperating with co-workers. Co-worker cooperation is like a baseball pool—you have to put something in to get something out. It's give and take.

The office affords a number of different ways of extending such cooperation.

EXCHANGING INFORMATION

A bookkeeper needing the date and number of a government regulation phoned a bookkeeper in another company to find out where she could obtain the data.

A secretary wanted to know where she could get the names of the members of the board of directors of some utility and railroad corporations. A friend in another office referred her to Moody's.

CONSIDERATION

The chief accountant sent a brochure about the company's annual report to the public relations director for approval.

After two days, the secretary to the public relations director, telephoned the accountant, "There'll be a little delay till I can send you an O.K." she informed him. "The president wants to look over the brochure, too."

The secretary not only showed consideration by letting the accountant know what happened to his brochure. She also removed any possible impression that the public relations director was holding the material on his desk without action.

COURTESY

A purchasing agent had a paper to notarize after five o'clock. The notary in the cashier's office had already left for the day. But the treasurer's assistant was still in her office. "I'll ask her to do it," the purchasing agent's clerk said to her boss.

The treasurer's assistant was none too cordial, since she was in a rush to get off some reports, but she notarized the papers.

The next morning the clerk typed a note for the purchasing agent's signature. It read:

DEAR MISS ROTHSCHILD:

When someone barges in at five o'clock with an affidavit to notarize, it's quite an imposition!

Therefore, I doubly appreciate your courtesy and cooperation in taking care of my papers last evening, when my clerk came in with them.

Thank you for helping me out in this emergency.

Sincerely,

PURCHASING AGENT.

When the treasurer's assistant met the clerk later in the day, she smiled pleasantly.

"Thank you" notes and other expressions of appreciation are always appropriate.

OFFERING A HELPING HAND

"Helping out a fellow worker who's in a bigger jam than you are is commendable (unless you had orders to the contrary), and she will probably help you back when you need it," says the *Handbook of Office Behavior* published by the Eaton Paper Company.[1]

To what extent to help others is a problem in most offices. "Nothing riles me more," Paula is bitter, "than to see other people in the department idle while my own work piles up."

Linda, in the same department, wonders, "Should I ask the supervisor for more work when I have free time? Should I go directly to one of the girls like Paula, who isn't as fast as the others?"

Many people prefer to struggle through their work alone. They feel that if they let others help them, it reflects on their ability to handle their job. Others fear that if they get into

[1] *A Handbook of Office Behavior.* Pittsfield, Mass.: Eaton Paper Corporation, 1950.

the habit of accepting help, they may be unexpectedly left high and dry if assistance is suddenly withdrawn.

You may find your offers of help rejected if you boast about it when you "come to the rescue." In an attempt to let others know you are a good sport, you may say, "Marie could never have gotten out on time last night if I hadn't done those envelopes for her." Marie overhears it, and is annoyed that news of the small amount of help you gave her is broadcast throughout the office.

Another angle to the problem of accepting help was expressed by a clerk. "Of course, you could help me," she thanked a co-worker, "but if I finish all these vouchers today, my boss won't really know how much there is involved in this job. So I'd rather stay a few minutes later and let him see me doing the work myself."

A secretary never forgave a junior typist who offered to copy a report for her. The young girl did such a neat, painstaking job, and set up the work so attractively, that the boss went out of his way to commend the junior typist for her fine work.

Helping others doesn't mean volunteering information or prying. A girl in an insurance office was accused of being a busybody. Her boss, who knew she was only trying to be helpful, told her: "Even if some advice from you will prevent a mistake, you'll have to let people find out for themselves if they are wrong, unless they definitely come to you. Just do your own work. Perhaps, after a few months, you will live down your reputation."

DOING YOUR SHARE OF THE WORK

The following is a letter received by the newspaper columnist, Mrs. Emily Post:

I work in a fairly large office and heretofore a few of us at a time would go downstairs to the drugstore for a cup of coffee.

Some of the girls abused this privilege and the management has requested us not to go down any more. However, one of the young women still goes down without the management knowing it. At the end of the day she is behind in her work because of this and the rest of us have to help her. This is very irritating but none of us know what to do about it short of telling the office manager, which seems a "sneaky" thing to do.

This situation isn't unique. Every office seems to have a girl who disappears into the ladies room when there's mimeographing to be done, or who stays home the day after a holiday. Such girls get by a surprisingly long time, too, because their co-workers are too ethical to show them up. But they usually push their tactics too far, and the management notices it.

COMPETITION CAUSES CONFLICT

No matter how sincere our efforts to cooperate with our co-workers, problems arise when we are placed in competitive positions with them.

In an advertising agency, the director was in the habit of assigning two girls to do the same job, independent of each other, whenever he needed some research data. His objective was that one might turn up something the other had overlooked.

When they were finished, he would call them into his office together and compare their respective reports.

Pitting the girls—and other people in the office—against each other in this way, caused everyone to be at "sword's points."

Finally, a girl had the courage to point out to him that this method of operation meant considerable duplication. "Why not let people work together in teams and hand in joint reports?" she asked.

The results have proved the wisdom of her suggestion.

Girls in stenography pools, or secretaries who share bosses, must take extra precautions so they will not develop non-cooperative attitudes.

The general sales manager and the head of the market research division of a company jointly had two secretaries. This arrangement was feasible because the general sales manager was frequently away on extended trips, and did not need a full-time girl. When he returned, however, he kept both girls busy for a short period. The market research head, on the other hand, had a steady flow of work for both girls, much of it statistical typing, which could be held up when the sales manager was in town.

One of the girls, Virginia, was extremely conscientious. The other girl, Beth, did as little work as possible. This made Virginia angry, so that she alternately complained to both men.

Everyone in the office was shocked when Virginia was asked to resign. The bosses justified their decision by saying, "Evidently the two girls can't get along."

Some men don't take the trouble to find out who's right in such a situation. They just follow the path of least resistance and get rid of the person who causes them inconvenience by reports of dissension, regardless of the merits of a case.

COOPERATING WITH THE BOSS

In some parts of Europe, it used to be the custom to set a newly married couple to work on a log with a two-man saw. It takes real cooperation to saw a log that way. The partners are not of equal strength, but they do have to work in harmony.

That is the type of harmony that should exist between a boss and those who work with him. Such a partnership results in a we-us relationship that makes every job a challenge.

How can we achieve partnership with the boss?

1. Help him realize his ambitions.

Ted Weber, head of the drafting department, was talking with Sarah. "What do you think is the best approach to the big boss to find out what plans he has in store for me? I seem to have gotten into a rut around here. I'd sure like to know where I'm going. Maybe I'll just talk to him and put the cards on the table."

Sarah had noticed that the chief engineer did not react well to a head-on approach. She advised Ted, "Why not make a list of some of the projects you would like to undertake which would benefit the company, and at the same time give you opportunity to do the things you like to do?"

Then, during the discussion, she adroitly drew out from Ted some of his hopes and ambitions. This clarified in his own mind what he was really after. On the basis of this conversation, he drafted a memo to the boss that was favorably received.

2. Check critically.

You've heard bosses say of girls in their office, "I trust her more than I do myself," or "If she says so, it's right." Such confidence is built up if you check all information with an "eagle eye" both as it leaves the office and as it arrives from other departments. It saves your boss hours of time, and relieves him from strain to know he can always depend on you.

3. Conserve your boss's time.

Don't rush in on him whenever you have a question, unless it needs an immediate answer. Write down questions as they come up. Then in a few minutes' interview, go over them with him all at one session. Don't detain him when he's on his way out. He will give you an off-hand answer that may have to be reversed later. And he'll be annoyed at the delay.

4. Be a clearing house for others.

Many times requests for information can stop short at a girl's desk if she sets herself up as a clearing house. Suppose a man wants the latest figures on a pension report from your boss. You tell him that your boss has already O.K.'d the report and passed it on to the insurance department. The man goes directly to the insurance department, preventing needless interruption.

5. Help him do "the impossible."

Occasionally, your boss may undertake a project which is beyond his accomplishment alone.

A business man had agreed to testify before a Senate Committee on short notice. The afternoon before he left for Washington, he received some data from a trade association which considerably strengthened his argument. "But it's too late," he remarked regretfully to his bookkeeper, "to recalculate our figures and incorporate this information." He took the brief "as is," and mentioned he was catching the nine o'clock plane the following morning.

After he left, she took a copy of his brief and the trade association data and went home. She revised the brief, finishing, after intermittent cups of coffee, at one o'clock in the morning. At 8:30 she was at the airport, and handed her boss the revised brief, which he studied on his way to Washington.

The presentation was highly commended for its thoroughness.

Such cooperation beyond the call of duty, results in a deeply rewarding sense of satisfaction.

Whenever you cooperate with a superior, you risk being accused of trying to "take over." In this respect, women have the advantage over men. They do not compete for their boss's job. This allows them freedom of action. Over a period of time, an executive will let a woman assume more authority and responsibility than he would ever think of delegating to a male assistant. When a boss feels that a girl is his "eyes and ears," or his "right hand," you can be assured she has mastered the art of unobtrusive cooperation.

CAUGHT IN THE CROSSFIRE

Cooperation with the boss may be complicated if you report to more than one person.

For example, a girl worked for both father and son who subconsciously were rivals. They argued about who was to give her dictation first in the morning. She was always in a quandary as to who should be given preference when she was pushed for time. Currently, the father was in authority. But her future would be with the son who was being groomed for the presidency.

Two partners in a sales office were in continuous conflict. They claimed each others' customers and countermanded each others' instructions. The receptionist didn't know to whom to hand the mail in the morning! She left it on her desk, and the partner who came in first picked it up and bore it to his office.

If you find yourself in a conflict situation, don't let trivialities bother you. Don't get involved in personalities—that is, don't take sides. Base your actions on what is best for the over-all good of the enterprise you work for.

YOU CAN BE TOO COMPLIANT AND WILLING

The girl who can't say "no" and judiciously discriminate when asked for assistance can be a disruptive influence.

1. Others feel she is taking their work away from them.

Several college professors in an English department of a college wrote illegibly. They suggested to the newly-appointed department secretary that she herself type the examinations they prepared, rather than send them to the typing pool, as in the past. The reason for their request was, "You understand our writing and are familiar with the content of the material."

She obligingly accommodated them. The typing pool girls wanted to know, "How come?" Typing of examinations was one of their specific assignments. They argued that they had been able to decipher the professors' handwriting satisfactorily in the past and should continue to do this work.

2. You may hold up your own work.

Mr. Nichols, the sales manager of a supply house often asked the secretaries of other executives to do some little jobs for him when his own girl was busy. He didn't stop to check with the executives whose girls he "borrowed." And the girls hesitated to bother their bosses by telling them, "I'm doing a half-hour job for Mr. Nichols." As a result, their own work was sometimes delayed.

In such a situation, don't be intimidated by the executive who enlists your help. You owe it to your boss to tell him the score. It's up to him—not to you—to decide to what extent he wants to cooperate with another man.

3. You may jeopardize your job status.

A capable and energetic young woman had been recommended by her supervisor to be an administrative assistant. The personnel director promised to have a talk with her and judge her qualifications.

Accordingly, a few days later, the personnel director came to her desk and asked for a summary she had prepared.

"We have no copies available, but I have the stencils," she answered eagerly. "I can run them off for you. I use the hand machine in the mail room to help out the duplicating department all the time."

Her promotion was refused. "She is not of administrative caliber if she spends so much time on a job like mimeographing, where her skills are not used at maximum effectiveness," was his conclusion.

No matter how generous your impulse to help others, you must learn to curb it so that such assistance does not take up a disproportionate amount of your working day.

CHAPTER VIII

The Purpose of Planning

HALF the fun in giving a party is in the planning. First, you must have a purpose for entertaining. You may feel socially obligated to repay people who have entertained you at their home. You may wish to introduce an out-of-town visitor to your friends. Or you may give a birthday party, farewell send-off or shower to honor someone. The purpose will determine whom you will invite, the kind of food you will serve, the games and entertainment you will provide. And if your party is a success, you get considerable satisfaction out of knowing your arrangements were carefully made.

The principles of planning for a party can be translated into planning in the office. Right here you may interject, "What would be the purpose of my planning? I have to do as I'm told!" But you instinctively know that isn't so! No woman exists who doesn't do some planning. And if her plans are for a more smoothly functioning office, she's bound to get her way.

Your planning should have two underlying purposes:

1. To help your boss plan his work by offering ideas or to assist him in organizing his activities methodically.
2. To analyze your own work so you will make the most effective use of your time and efforts.

PROGRAM FOR PLANNING

Planning implies that you approach your work in an orderly, step-by-step fashion.

THE TIME TABLE

You have a time table. In giving your party, you decide on the date and hour, how long ahead of time you will invite your guests, when you want ice cream and other perishables delivered.

In the office your Time Table has scores of applications:

1. Arrange to have your work ready at specified hours or days. Often this time table is set by your supervisor. For example, all payroll sheets may have to be finished by Tuesday night so that checks can be prepared.

If you are a good planner, you not only finish at the deadline, but you may have some time left to spare. Perhaps you feel there's no incentive to saving time. But you can be certain your supervisor or boss will soon notice your efficiency.

An interesting system is in effect at the Air Reduction Company, Inc., of New York. A clerk who finishes her work in less time than provided for by the standards "sells" available time to another job or another department. A simple form, called a "Time Journal," is used to record the time "sold." No extra compensation is given, but the girls who "sell" time automatically stand out for promotions.

2. Group your work to the extent that you have control over timing. You may have to plan for bills, announcements, bulletins to reach their destination on a certain date, as the first of the month, and must set up a spaced schedule for yourself. Press releases are "timed" to the hour.

The secretary's job lends itself to grouping. Surveys show that secretaries have some 871 different duties, although the average is about 132 different tasks. In an article, "These Secretaries Make Big Money," in the *Cosmopolitan*, secretaries to such men as Conrad N. Hilton, the hotel owner, Oscar Hammerstein II, theatrical producer, Frank Stanton, president of Columbia Broadcasting System, and Leroy A. Wilson, president of American Telephone and Telegraph Company, claim their duties stretch from handling mail and answering correspondence to selecting ties, making out income tax returns, buying toys for children, designing their bosses' offices and buying wedding wardrobes. Secretaries with such diversified duties generally make it a practice to accumulate dictation until there's about an hour's typing to do. They do the typing at one sitting, and follow through with proofreading. When possible, they make a series of outgoing telephone calls at one session. If they were to start and stop all the time, the interruptions would lower their efficiency.

The person who plans well doesn't let interruptions sidetrack her. As soon as possible, she returns to the routine she has laid out for herself.

3. Concentrate on what you are doing right at the moment. Some people have a tendency to worry about whether a letter is correctly addressed, whether figures on an invoice are accurately added, whether they have miscalculated someone's pay, or charged the wrong price for an item. While you're busy worrying, you don't think of what you are doing. Later, you'll start worrying whether you did the present job right—an endless cycle of anxiety.

4. Tackle the job ahead when you come to it, but do not go over it mentally half a dozen times before. If you keep dwelling on it, you double the burden, and are worn out just from dreading the task.

5. Remind your boss, others in the company, or yourself to attend to things at certain times. The appointment book— both your boss's and your own—is a good example of this type of time table.

6. Hunt up jobs on your own accord that you know must be done. If your boss forgets to give you some work, nothing is gained by playing ostrich and hoping, "Maybe he won't think

about it." It eliminates hurrying later if you help your boss
plan his work to have it ready when required.

7. Extend the time table to your personal life. With many
married women, it means they must shop, make phone calls,
take care of business details in connection with the home such
as paying bills, insurance premiums, or going to the bank
during their lunch hour. Divide such chores to give yourself
sufficient time to eat, plus a few moments to wash up and
put on new make-up.

THE BUDGET

In giving your party, you decide how much you want to
spend. You have a budget.

Budgets are familiar to us as financial devices in business.
We think of them as existing in the office of the treasurer or
controller, but we usually don't visualize the relationship between our own job and the budget.

The cost of running his department reflects on the success
of your boss or your supervisor. Departmental budgets are
based on the cost of payroll dollars, the cost of supplies and
maintenance.

1. The cost of payroll dollars.

To help our boss meet his budget, we must spend our working hours profitably. And in the end, this gives us greater
satisfaction. The most bored people are those who try to find
ways of "killing time." Some ways and means are:

A. Combine tasks. If you go to another department, you
   can cut down backtracking if on the same trip you
   collect supplies that may be needed soon. Even useless
   trips by the office boy cost money.

B. Ask questions about information you need all at one
   time. Don't call back the Purchasing Department, for
   example, half a dozen times for the date, the amount,
   the destination, the price, of a certain order.

C. Try to avoid errors and mistakes. Most costly of all items on the office budget is the time spent in checking inaccuracies in figures, hunting for lost or misfiled papers and recopying reports or letters.

A methods man in an eastern company studied 15,000 different forms and arrived at the conclusion that twenty to twenty-five dollars' worth of work was put on every dollar's worth of paper. *Business Education World* estimates that the average cost of a letter is $1.17. It's not hard to figure out how much "doing over" adds to these already high amounts.

D. Help reduce your departmental budget by keeping a sharp lookout for unnecessary forms or duplication of work.

E. Suggest destroying obsolete records. Studies made by the National Records Management Council show that approximately 80 per cent of all business records should have a life span of ten years or less. Fewer than 10 per cent of business records are permanent.

The Records Management Association and the Office Management Division of the American Management Association, both of New York, publish helpful booklets on this subject.

2. The cost of supplies.

Many people want considerably more office supplies on hand than they actually need at any one time. Next to salaries, the major item of office expense is, generally, not the mechanical equipment and furniture, but the supply items required from day to day. The cost of paper, carbons, stencils, cleaning fluid, erasers, pencils, ribbons, paste, file folders, envelopes and paper clips may easily average $5 per day per office employee. Where punch cards, multi-carbon snap-on forms, or specially printed ledger sheets are used, it runs much higher.

In these cost-conscious days, it is an unwritten part of your job description to keep the cost of supplies at a minimum.

3. Maintenance.

The equipment you use, which depreciates or becomes obsolete, costs the company another $4 per day on the average. Proper maintenance of such equipment is a responsibility of the "office housekeeper." In many companies, typewriters, comptometers, adding machines and accounting machines are periodically serviced. But if you have equipment that is not so automatically taken care of, take a tip from car lubrication. Place a sticker on your machine with the date you last cleaned or oiled it, or called for service.

The List

A shopping list is a prerequisite in arranging your party. A list is likewise essential for efficient office planning. Do not confuse a list with the time table, although the functions of the two sometimes overlap. A list is a guide, or reminder.

1. One type of list typical of the office is the procedure manual. This may range from simple instructions on such matters as alphabetizing, number of copies of forms or letters required, routing of correspondence. Or it may be a complete guide of office organization with titles of offices and executives, location of departments and extensive rules and regulations.

2. Notes or memos are in reality lists in another form. In describing Margaret A. Brown, secretary to the president of Sohio, it was said that "in addition to the president's appointment book, Miss Brown maintains her own personal calendar, every page of which is full of notations of things to do. Attached to these are slips of paper of all sizes and shapes, notes from the president, from his assistant, from secretaries in other departments and notes from Miss Brown to herself— some of them scribbled while she was at home or on the rapid transit to or from work."

3. Some girls find it helpful to list their unfinished jobs at

the end of the day. When they open their desk in the morning, they glance over the list and give precedence to the things that are most important, rather than picking a job at random without any plan for the day's work.

4. It's also good policy to keep a list of reserve jobs. These include filing, indexing, retyping the telephone directory, cleaning out cabinets—all to be done when you're not busy. Most of us put off jobs which aren't urgent. But they catch up with us at the unlikeliest moments.

5. Take an inventory to see that booklets, enclosures and maps are available in the store room. The supply clerk does not always automatically re-order unless you tell him whether the material will continue to be used.

THE BLUEPRINT

Your party calls for a seating plan around the table—maybe placecards. You arrange your dishes, silver, glasses according to a pattern. Furniture must be grouped around the television set or cleared away for dancing. Mentally, you have a blueprint of your home in mind when making your arrangements.

In business, we associate blueprints with the drafting room. But the same principles of arrangement apply to our daily operations in the office.

1. Supplies frequently used should be kept in accessible places.

2. Files should be so arranged, as far as feasible, that material continually referred to is readily available. Perhaps you can keep some folders in front of the file, with a guide card temporarily inserted to show that such folders or cards are out of sequence.

3. Check the path you take on trips to the wash room, the boss's office, the water cooler, other departments, or to get supplies. You've noticed how people tend to take the same seat in the bus every day, provided it is vacant, even if it may be

harder to get off at their destination than if they chose a more convenient seat. In the same way we form the habit of taking circuitous routes in the office. Perhaps originally the desks were placed differently, or we have a friend whom we wanted to pass, or the aisles were wider. Taking the shortest distance between two points not only saves time, but reduces our own fatigue.

SUMMARY

Planning is organized activity accomplished by techniques such as the time table, the budget, the list and the blueprint. We need such a pattern of procedure to enable us to control our efforts effectively.

CHAPTER IX

Adventures in Initiative

THE J. Walter Thompson Company, advertising agency, includes on its application for employment such questions as:

"Have you initiative?"

"Imagination?"

"Do you do your best work when it is planned for you or when you plan it for yourself?"

"Of what part of your work are you most proud?"

"What one thing do you think you contributed while at your previous job which improved or developed either it or the method of handling it?"

These questions are obviously aimed at discovering initiative. Initiative puts adventure into our work.

Girls in offices inherently possess a high degree of initiative —otherwise they wouldn't choose office work to begin with. You can make your own job if you work in an office—but you must use initiative.

FOLLOW THE LEADER

How can we describe initiative? Perhaps you remember when you were in school you played a game called, "Follow the Leader." A child who was not afraid to start things was chosen as leader. The others fell in line behind her. She made certain motions which the others imitated—waving her arms, jumping over imaginary hurdles, anything her fertile little brain could devise. This leader had initiative.

Initiative is finding things to do and having the courage to do them.

FINDING WHAT TO DO

Two girls in a subway were discussing their bosses. One of them burst out defiantly, "He's so unfair! He told me I have no initiative! Why, I always do everything he tells me to do!"

This girl had no conception of initiative. Initiative requires doing more than the job calls for—using ingenuity and inventiveness to make the most of every opportunity at hand.

At first Anita, assigned to a stenography pool, did not see how she could show much initiative. It was plain she had no control over the work she was called on to do. But she decided to make the best of the circumstances.

After a few weeks, more and more men specified to the transcription supervisor, "I prefer Anita." Anita was accurate, dependable, pleasant. In addition, if a letter she transcribed mentioned, for example, "I will telephone you about this next week," she attached a reminder memo to the dictator so he would not forget to make the call. She invented all sorts of little personalized services. Anita was soon promoted because she had initiative.

There are three ways by which we can develop initiative.

Use Imagination

An executive was gratified at the way a girl had followed through on his rather sketchy instructions. "You practically read my mind," he complimented her. "It seems to me that if I got on the phone with you at the other end and I concentrated for a few minutes, you would know what I wanted without my ever speaking a word."

Outguessing the boss by anticipating his needs ranks first in the personal qualifications of an executive secretary, a survey by Rohrer, Hibler and Replogle, a management consultant firm, reveals. One boss replying to the survey said, "My secretary instinctively knows what I'm going to do next." Opportunities to "outguess" the boss come up every day.

In a large steel mill, the air was charged with excitement. Everyone was on the alert. The research assistant to the industrial relations manager, however, did not let herself be distracted by all the hubbub and discussions in the ante-room. She calmly read about the procedures the company must take in the event of a strike; what government authorities must be notified; how many guards would be required; how the foremen should proceed. When the work-force walked out, operations were shut down with a minimum of confusion. This girl's foresight saved the company several thousand dollars.

In an air conditioning plant, the vice president was scheduled to visit several cities to address management meetings. On the eve of his departure, a typist in his office handed him a record of the company's customers in the respective towns he would visit. She included the names of top executives, what wholesaler they dealt with, and other pertinent facts. "Just in case you should run into some of these men," she offered the list hesitatingly. The information proved so helpful that he never traveled without similar preparation in the future.

Suggestions in memorandum form which your boss can use as a basis for dictation or other action, are a subtle way of showing initiative.

"This chap Jim Carter went to college with me. He's married, has two teen-age sons," a stockbroker commented to his secretary as he frowningly scanned a letter with a postmark from India. "He represents several shipping agencies in Bombay. Now he wants to throw up his job and come to the United States. He wonders whether he can get something that will pay him enough so his family can live in comfortable style in America. What can I tell him?" With a futile gesture of resignation, he pushed the letter to the bottom of the pile.

The secretary tried to imagine what she would do if she were in India faced with a similar problem. Then she drew up some suggestions and attached them to Carter's letter to help her boss when he dictated a reply to his friend.

Because executives are frequently contacted by their friends, fraternity brothers, people from the "home town," or business associates in connection with changing jobs, this girl's memo is presented because it can easily be adapted to similar cases. This is what she wrote:

MEMO RE: JIM CARTER

1. It would handicap Mr. Carter in his search for a job if he gives up his present connection before making a new one.

2. Therefore, he should temporarily stay in India, but plan an active job-hunting campaign from his base in Bombay. The foreign stamp on his correspondence will be an attention-attracting asset.

3. He should prepare a resumé of his background. He should state frankly why he wishes to leave India (to give his sons an American education.) The attached advertisements from *The New York Times* describe agencies that prepare professional job resumés.

4. Mr. Carter should write the Bureau of Foreign and Domestic Commerce in Washington, D. C., for information about companies that might reasonably be interested in someone of his experience.

5. Mr. Carter should send a resumé with accompanying letter to about fifty selected contacts. He should state that his present business is making it imperative for him to be in the United States during the month of ——. He should mention he will be glad to present himself if the company in question would like to discuss his availability. This approach will not obligate potential employers. Hence, they will feel free to make an appointment which they might otherwise hesitate to do.

With this memo before him, it didn't take the stockbroker long to dictate an appropriate letter.

The president of a western lumber mill was to lunch with Mr. Davis, the attorney who was handling a law suit for the mill. They arranged to meet at the attorney's office and then go to a nearby country club together.

Just before noon, Mr. Benton, the lawyer for the defendant in the case, dropped in on Mr. Davis unannounced. His call had nothing to do with the lumber mill case. It just happened that both men were local Scout executives.

When the lumber mill president arrived, the receptionist realized he would inevitably meet Mr. Benton, the defendant's lawyer, now in the inner office with her boss, just as soon as the door opened. He might easily misconstrue the call, and suspect that the two attorneys were in collusion discussing the case. Quickly she said,

"Mr. Davis has had a slight change in plans. He would like to meet you right away at the country club."

After the president left, she phoned inside to her boss to tell him what she had done. He was relieved that she had the initiative to take steps to avoid needless embarrassment.

USE INTELLIGENCE

"I wish I had known, when I first started to work, [a secretary in a Detroit automobile plant recalled,] that you have to use your head even about the simplest things. Like the calendar . . .

"Soon after I came to Mr. Perry's office, I noticed he turned over the page of his calendar each night before he left for home. He'd glance over his engagements for the next day. So I never bothered about the calendar.

"Then one day around noon a very angry gentleman telephoned. It seems Mr. Perry had accepted an invitation to address a group of visitors being entertained by a service club.

Right then, they were finishing dessert, waiting for the speaker. Where was Mr. Perry, he wanted to know.

" 'There's nothing on his calendar!' I retorted. The man's annoyance increased because my boss had apparently forgotten the engagement.

"After he hung up, I was horrified to see that the calendar was opened to Wednesday, the nineteenth. Today was Tuesday, the eighteenth! Mr. Perry had flipped over two pages, and had not seen the memo about the speech. Since then, I check the calendar myself."

We all bring a certain amount of intelligence to our job. On top of that, the company makes an investment in developing our intelligence. The Los Angeles Merchants and Manufacturers Association estimates that the cost of training an office employee is between $169 and $342 per person. The purpose of such training is to help increase efficiency, avoid errors and create individual initiative.

There are almost no limits to the opportunities where we can apply intelligence.

Break It Up. "Please make-half-a-dozen copies of this telegram from the home office," the office manager in an insurance branch told one of the stenographers. "I want to distribute these instructions to our supervisors."

The telegram was a solid paragraph:

ALL CLAIMS MUST BE FILED (A) AT THE DISTRICT OFFICE ON OR BEFORE AUGUST 15 STOP (B) AT THE STATE OFFICE ON OR BEFORE AUGUST 20 STOP (C) AT THE NATIONAL OFFICE BEFORE AUGUST 25.

In typing these copies, the stenographer set them up as:

All claims must be filed:
(A) At the District Office on or before August 15
(B) At the State Office on or before August 20
(C) At the National Office *before* August 25.

When she brought the copies to the office manager she offered, "I'll be glad to do these over if that isn't what you want," in case he resented the initiative she had taken in breaking up the copy.

"Much easier to read!" he approved. "This shows you have real intelligence."

Successful Sleuthing. The assistant to the president brought in to a typist a list of names for which envelopes were to be typed.

The typist noticed that in most instances, the titles, such as Mayor, Editor, Senator, as well as all initials, were included. In a few isolated cases, however, complete information was lacking.

She used the telephone book, and other sources available to her, to supply the missing details. Her care made a good impression on the man for whom she did the work.

Job Inventory. A junior accountant has set up what she calls her "Job Inventory" file. Whenever she does something beyond her routine duties, she makes a record on a card. These cards remind her to be on the lookout for similar cases in the future where she can take independent action.

As she riffled the cards she said:

"On the first of every month, I send to the industrial relations manager a record of daily absences. On April sixteenth, as I posted his sheet, I noticed that absenteeism in the plant had reached a new low. I telephoned him, and he got out a bulletin to the factory congratulating the workers on their fine record. If I had merely given him the sheet at the end of the month, he might have overlooked this low figure. At any event, the memo to the workers would have been a post mortem."

Glancing at another card, she commented:

"The Knott Company buys coal from us, usually telephoning in an order for fifty tons. One day I saw an order for five hundred tons. The girl who took down the information insisted she had made no mistake. So I got in touch with our sales department. The error had occurred at Knott's. They were grateful that we verified this unusual order."

She continued, "A machine that breaks down too often, a new high in sales, reports that don't arrive when due . . . these are the type of things that should be called to someone's attention. I just always make sure to differentiate between information that can be furnished without clearance and that which needs the approval of the controller."

SHOW INTEREST

The story is told of a typist who felt she was at the bottom of some 3000 employees in an insurance company. One day a suggestion contest was announced. She submitted three ideas about her work. When she heard that only fifty people in all had sent in suggestions, she felt she stood a little higher on the ladder.

Then one of her ideas won a prize. Now she was someone! She counted! Ten years later, she had risen to department head with 400 girls under her supervision. This girl started on the way up to success because she had interest in what she was doing.

Interest may be shown in a wide variety of ways.

Perhaps another company sends you a bill, a report, or other form that seems to be better than the one you are using. Do you call it to the attention of your boss? You may notice a letter set up differently. We recently received one that read:

> Mr. George Conners
> The Foundation Company
> Chicago, Illinois

> Thank you Mr. Conners
>   for your estimate of June 10th.

Maybe your boss is conservative and disapproves of such in-novations. That's not the point. The question is, have you tried to show your interest?

At a publishing house, it was customary to leave outgoing telegrams with the telephone operator, where the Western Union boy picked them up. The operator was on duty till 5:30—half an hour after the office officially closed.

One morning the editor saw a wire he had sent out the night before still in the basket. "This should have gone out yesterday! Now I won't even be able to get this author on the phone because he's left on a camping trip by this time."

The operator looked up innocently. "It isn't my fault. I rang Western Union but they didn't come." It never occurred to her that she should have telephoned the wire, or dropped it off at the Western Union office on her way home.

Sometimes we don't see things that are right before our eyes. If we learn to be keen observers, it not only sharpens our intelligence but makes a good impression on those with whom we come in contact.

A visitor had an appointment with Mrs. Daly. He knew he would subsequently want to write her a thank you note for the interview she was granting him.

"Could you tell me how you spell Mrs. Daly's name and her initials, please?" he asked the girl at the reception desk as he waited.

"I don't know, but I'll try to find out." She came back with the information. "I think it's D-a-l-y. Her first name is Rose."

A few minutes later he turned around and noticed on the door in back of where he was sitting the name Rosa Daley. Then it flashed on him that the receptionist must look at that door a hundred times a day, since she faced in that direction.

She didn't have sufficient interest in her job to learn the names of those with whom she was associated.

Some girls are so shy and diffident that they don't know how to go about showing interest.

"My boss never has a minute to himself. Telephone calls all day long," Nadine described her office. That doesn't speak well for her. It means she isn't doing a topnotch job. A good secretary is a buffer for her boss.

Nadine argues that her boss has made it plain he wants to talk to everyone himself. "My boss was that way too," said Myra, her friend. "He never let me take any calls. Then, one day, I decided he just didn't have enough confidence in my ability to handle his business."

"How did you change him?" Nadine was curious.

"I made it a point to take an interest in everything that goes on. For instance, one day the printer sent over some proofs. Ordinarily, I'd hand them to Mr. Kerner and let it go at that. This day, I went into his office about half an hour later and asked, 'Are the proofs O.K.?' He answered, 'They're all right.'

"In the afternoon, when the printer phoned, instead of switching the call to Mr. Kerner, I went in to him. 'Acme Printing wants to know whether the proofs have been approved. I'll tell them you've O.K.'d them, can't I? That will save you talking with them.'

"When he realized that I would give the proper information over the telephone, and was capable of handling the calls, he let me take more and more initiative."

Another instance where a girl did not know how to express her interest came to light in a Texas city.

Ben Cowden, personnel director of a cash-and-carry chain of thirty-five markets, had this experience. About a year ago, he was in the midst of union negotiations. On top of that, a new pension system had been installed. The president thought a house organ would improve morale. Ben was appointed editor. There was just one stipulation—it shouldn't cost much.

Ben related his story. "I felt I could turn out a fairly good paper if I had a little help. But as it was, I sat home nights, cutting out pictures and pasting up a dummy. Ruth, the girl in my office, didn't make any attempt to relieve me of my burden.

"One day I was attracted by a fairly creditable high school magazine on her desk, and asked whether her picture was in it. She seemed reluctant to let me look at the magazine. 'I just brought it in to show to one of the girls. It's not very good— I used to be the editor,' she apologized.

"I was dumbfounded," Ben concluded. "Here I had talent right in my office. It developed that Ruth was just 'dying' to work on the house organ, but felt she wouldn't be good enough. Now she practically runs the whole thing."

In the majority of cases, however, interest in the job is apparent right from the start.

In a drafting office in Chicago, two girls began as typists about three years ago. Kate fell into the routine—so much and no more. Phyllis, on the other hand, listened with marked interest to the conversations between the engineers. She looked up in the dictionary words she didn't understand. She was always willing to take down notes at staff meetings, staying late or postponing her lunch hour. She studied magazines like Mechanical Engineering, Power, Mill and Factory. Today she is secretary to the plant engineer.

What's more, such interest continues, even if girls leave their jobs.

Charlotte, a clerk in charge of health, safety and insurance statistics in an industrial plant, resigned because she was pregnant. She appreciated what her successor would be up against with all the details this job involved. So she prepared a large scrapbook, pasting in all the forms, and writing out procedures and instructions. The manager of the department was so impressed that he showed the scrapbook to the vice president.

Shortly after Charlotte's baby was born, her husband was killed. She was forced to support her child. Her former job was capably filled—partly because she had given her successor such a good start.

The vice president, however, remembered the scrapbook. He found a better place for her in the organization than she formerly held. Charlotte's interest in what would happen to her job after she was gone accrued to her advantage.

Finding things to do relieves our job of monotony. "Digging out" new assignments may add some extra duties which we may have to fit in with our regular work for a while, until the value of what we have created is recognized. But sooner or later initiative results in changing our jobs into the type of work we like to do.

FIND THE COURAGE TO DO IT

We can all find things to do if we use imagination, intelligence and show interest. But many of us lack the courage to carry through our projects. We frequently hear people say, "I didn't do anything because I was afraid it would be wrong." This is a rationalization to cover up their lack of courage, although they are seldom aware of it. One executive always countered this excuse by telling his staff members that "the worst offense is to do nothing."

How can we fortify ourselves with courage?

1. We must decide that we will not let group pressure deter us from action. Highest examples of courage are invariably found on the battlefield. The hero knows that his courage

will be universally applauded—that his fellow soldiers, his officers, and the folks back home are with him. But in the business world, courage may face ridicule. Your co-workers intimate that you are "polishing the apple," or that you are "a company girl." Women in particular are instinctively influenced by group attitudes.

Eleanor was the most recently hired stenographer-clerk in a government agency. She had scarcely begun her duties when the other girls in the office gave her "advice." "Don't start work before nine, even if your train gets you here earlier." "Don't help with the filing—that's not in your job description." "Don't bother to read the directives," and "Don't stay to finish your work because you don't get paid unless your overtime is officially approved."

Eleanor resisted this regimentation imposed by her co-workers. She realized, however, that if she antagonized the group, she would be ostracized. So she went along with the taboos that had been set up and she openly conformed to the accepted behavior.

But she did not let the group attitude inhibit her. One day while taking dictation, she suggested to the director a new method of indexing the directives to facilitate his work. He assigned this indexing to Eleanor, so in the course of her duties she had to read everything that came into the office. This familiarized her with the work of the agency. Week by week, unobtrusively, she changed the scope of her work.

When the assistant director, a man, left, Eleanor was promoted to his job. Her knowledge of the work was one reason for this advancement. But almost of equal importance was the fact that she had retained the good will of the other clerks.

Pressure from an individual may keep us from exercising initiative.

"Sometimes my boss asks me to call up a customer for him," Harriet, the only girl in a construction firm, related. "His assistant is offended. He feels he should be the one to make such calls." The assistant's attitude was the reason why Harriet was slowly stifling her initiative.

"I don't mind as long as the boss gives me a specific assignment. But I'm extra careful never to do anything on my own. I don't want to step on the assistant's toes."

An individual sometimes can intimidate us more easily than a group. If we lose his—or her—good will, we seem to be entirely defenseless. The solution, just as in the previous case, is to direct our initiative into channels that are not in obvious conflict with the other person's.

2. A second approach to developing courage is to ask ourselves, "Do things happen to me, or do I make them happen?"

A French novelist wrote that whenever anything occurs in our lives we have already gone more than half way to anticipate it. This philosophy holds good in practical, everyday situations, as is indicated by the advice given by a newspaper columnist, Anne Heywood. A girl wrote to her:

So many women are urged to take secretarial jobs as an entering wedge. This is what I have done and I'm afraid I'm stuck with it.

I have been with my firm for five years and there has never been any chance to move away from straight secretarial work into personnel interviewing, as I was promised. I'm still taking dictation and doing typing for the personnel director.

The columnist replied as follows:

It's been my experience that when a secretary doesn't get promoted as promised in the original agreement, it is due to one of three things: (1) She hasn't been doing a good job, and they doubt her capacity to do a higher-up job. (2) She is doing an adequate job secretarially but has shown no initiative in digging up extra assignments for herself which would lead to promotion. (3) The company doesn't mean their promise.

Let's discuss points one and two. Too many girls take secretarial jobs as a means to an end but do a very bad job. Because they are dreaming of the day when they will not be doing straight shorthand, they live in the future. The answer is to do the present job the best you can, because, only in so doing, can you make enough impression so the company will consider promoting you.

Point two is a little more subtle, and is, I should imagine, the difficulty with the girl who wrote me.

Sometimes opportunity doesn't drop in our lap. Sometimes we have to rustle it up. For example she might study the company's application blank to see if she could make it more effective, or briefer, or less distasteful to the applicant to fill out. Or she might express hunches about some of the applicants when they first appear, and build up a reputation of being right in her appraisal of people.

If you are in a secretarial job, and want to emerge from it, it takes just two things: First do your present job perfectly, and second, load the dice in your favor by taking upon yourself extra jobs in a non-secretarial capacity which will give you a chance to merit that desired promotion.

This columnist's advice is directed to secretaries. In principle, it applies to all office jobs if we want to meet the future half way. We must ask ourselves:

"Do I think beyond my job?"

"Do I make my services of the greatest value?"

"Do I explore what positions ahead have to offer?"

"Do I make an effort to get the knowledge and experience required to fill those positions?"

"Do I have the courage to take action when the opportunity presents itself? Or am I afraid to take the risk that greater responsibility brings?"

CHAPTER X

Let Machines Help You Develop

"No DOUBT, American women feel that all work should be done by machinery, as far as possible. They would be foolish if they did not."

Is this the opinion of a girl in a modern office? No, it is from a section on "Employment," in a book called *Common Sense about Women*, published in 1882.[1] If women were enthusiastic about machines then, they have reason to be a hundred times more so today, because women have invariably taken over occupations when they become mechanized.

The first practical typewriter was put on the market in the 1870's. It was operated by women from the beginning. Other types of office machines were invented later, and these, too, were run largely by women. These machines, and particularly the typewriter, in the operation of which women showed so much adaptability and skill, began the custom of the presence of at least one woman in practically every office.

In 1870 the number of women in offices was a mere fraction compared to the present day—some 13,500 against nearly six million—about 440 times as many. Only about 900 women were bookkeepers, accountants and cashiers in 1870. Men were forty times as numerous. Now more than half of the book-keepers are women with the total number of women in this phase of office work close to half a million.

[1] Thomas W. Higginson. *Common Sense about Women*. Boston: Lee & Shepard, 1882.

Clerical work on the whole is increasing. In 1870 only one of every 160 employees was in clerical work. In 1915, 15 out of every 100 workers were employees in offices. Now the proportion has risen to 26 out of every 100. Office employees, during the past fifty years, increased at a rate of nearly three times as fast as the increase in the nation's total work force. As factories become more automatic, their output goes up. More output must be translated into more purchases, sales and corresponding paper work.

Today, many financial, insurance and institutional concerns do nothing but handle records. Clerical work is their only productive operation.

This period of tremendous expansion of clerical work coincided with the installation of cash registers, check writers, comptometers, bookkeeping machines, dictating machines, electric and multi-unit automatic typewriters, electric tabulating and punch card accounting, intercom and public address systems, duplicating and offset machines, letter openers, letter folding and sealing machines and postage meters. Some are as simple as the stapler. Others are as complicated as the Univac which can do, in a few hours, work that requires years of mathematical computation.

One would think that such labor-saving technological improvements would have reduced the number of clerical workers. Nevertheless, despite the introduction of these machines the number of clerical workers has increased more rapidly than any other occupational group as a result of the growing complexity of business.

1. Paper work is multiplying because of:
   A. Changes in the method of doing business through the increase of credit buying, sub-contracting and installment purchases.
   B. A marked trend toward expansion in industry. A greater variety and larger number of products are

manufactured and sold. More extensive markets are served.

2. Government regulation of business requires all kinds of government reports—income tax and social security reports, Securities and Exchange Commission questionnaires and the like.

3. Companies have become so large that top executives have to depend on written records for guidance. They can no longer carry the facts of their business in their heads. As this trend continues, we will need even more people engaged in communications, fact-gathering and compilation to enable business to function effectively.

MACHINES INCREASE OPPORTUNITIES FOR WOMEN

We have already seen that machines have been a major factor in creating jobs for women numerically. Machines have also enabled women to make comparatively faster progress in reaching top jobs in offices than they have in other fields. Ninety-four per cent of all secretaries are women. In the home office of an insurance company, it is reported that women hold one out of every five of the higher level positions.

Women have the edge in banks, which are highly mechanized. The American Institute of Banking reveals that currently about 60 per cent of the nation's 400,000 bank employees are women. They occupy every job from messengers to vice presidents.

Modern career girls are rising to the upper brackets of business, according to a report made by two Harvard and Boston University professors and Soundscriber Corporation. "Today's career girl is moving steadily toward higher responsibility and increased authority," is their conclusion. "She may be boss yet."

On the other hand, in factories only four out of a hundred women are officials. Women represent less than 5 per cent of any high grade professional group such as doctors, dentists, engineers, chemists, architects, lawyers or politicians.

Machines help women advance in office jobs because

1. The simplicity of the machine permits even new employees to do expert work faster—almost immediately.
2. Machines do the repetitive aspects of the work. This leaves women free to exercise the functions of analysis, judgment, inspection, decision and evaluation.

Women often complain of discrimination in business. They feel that men are preferred for executive jobs. One of the secrets is that men who rise to high positions do not hesitate to delegate work to others so that their minds are free for policy-making and creative work. Women will have to learn to emulate men in this respect if they want more responsibility. The first step is to delegate work. Since they usually have no assistants to call upon, the way men do, they can let machines do as much of their work as possible.

PURCHASING MACHINES

Directly or indirectly, you participate in purchasing office machines. If you are a secretary, a survey finds that your preference is asked in two out of three cases. Thirty-eight per cent of secretaries do the actual buying of office equipment and supplies—which amounts to about $3,100 apiece.

You will notice that advertisements are designed to appeal to you because market research shows that you are the buyer. One dictating machine company in its literature appropriately suggests, "Let your secretary see this machine in action—at the same time you do—and then ask her opinion." Another company advises, "Tell *him he* wants this machine . . . and you do, too!" A calculator company speaks of "A beautiful partnership—party of the first part *me* . . . party of the second part *my* machine."

OUR ATTITUDE TOWARD THE MACHINE

The girl in the office can sabotage the machine or make it a success. We have already seen that machines open up opportunities for employment and for advancement on a broad scale. Now we want to see how the machine affects our immediate individual jobs. To find some of the answers, we asked questions of girls in Los Angeles, in Washington, D.C., in New York City, and in many places in between. There is no doubt that American women are brought up to be gadget-minded. At home they have sewing machines, cake mixers, electric percolators, and scores of other devices. They have no fear of mastering any kind of skill a machine may require. Girls who were taught office machines in business schools and in college expect to find the modern office mechanized.

Why, then, did we encounter some resistance when machines were introduced in offices where they affected the established procedures? The most prevalent reaction was, "We'll lose contact with the boss."

A payroll department was converted to punch cards. The girls objected and grumbled. This was not because they were forced to use machines—they had been working on comptometers before. It was not because the machines were more tiring. The new machines were self-checking, so the girls didn't have to worry about accuracy any more. Their real concern was that these new machines operated with almost automatic precision.

"Before, we were at the supervisor's desk whenever we didn't balance, or when mistakes occurred. Now, we have no reason to move about. There just aren't any mistakes."

These girls missed the personal contact with the supervisor. They did not perceive that hitherto, such contact was on a negative basis, admittedly confined to complaints, errors, delays. Now their job would provide a challenge. In order to gain attention, they would have to make suggestions for improving procedures, methods of gathering information, flow of work, requisitioning of materials.

Since drudgery had been taken out of their work, they would have the time to think of suggestions, too! When they were sold on the idea that positive action would bring them the desired contact, and would simultaneously lay the way for advancement, they were more inclined toward acceptance of the machines. It is not inconsistent that a business machines company has as its slogan, THINK.

Our survey was particularly directed to the reaction of secretaries to the dictating machine.

"I know dictation wastes time," a Radio City secretary in a broadcasting studio conceded, *"but when I'm sitting in my boss's office, I overhear important conversations, or meet celebrities. That makes my job exciting. I'd miss a lot of this if I were at my desk all day transcribing."*

The secretary to a well-known commentator cut in, "I thought that, too, but let me tell you how things worked out. Mr. T. never likes to be interrupted when he's working. But when I was inside with him taking notes, people simply walked past the door and broke into the conversation. Now, they don't get past me when he's dictating to the machine. The result is many of them take up their business with me direct, rather than come back to see him. So I'm in closer contact with prominent people than ever before. And because I no longer have to be on call when an idea strikes him, Mr. T. now sends me out to interview guests for the program."

Downtown in a New York utility the assistant to the chief statistician said, "My boss relied on me for supplying him with facts and figures. Dictation with us was a two-way process. He'd stop in the middle of a sentence and inquire, 'Myrtle.

where did we get such-and-such data?' And I'd answer him, giving specific sources of information. Often he'd compliment me on my good memory.

"Then one day he had to stay home with a broken leg," she continued. "Since I couldn't be both places at once, we got a machine on trial. Every morning I wert to his house with the current assignments. He'd spend the rest of the day dictating the answers.

"But, this meant I had to analyze the material ahead of time, anticipate what data he might need, supply him with information beforehand, instead of on the spur of the moment, as had previously been the case. My boss felt I was smarter than ever! What's more, once I had all the data collected, I discovered that I could often prepare some of the answers myself!"

A legal stenographer also admitted this innate desire for praise. "It gave me a real thrill when my boss would say, 'Am I going too fast for you?' and I'd shake my head, 'No, I got it all.' Or when I had to read back long paragraphs, especially in front of a client, and I'd have it letter perfect!"

What had converted her? "My brother is always boasting about his driving skill," she explained. 'Drove to Syracuse in six hours,' he announced at supper one night. The family as usual oh'd and ah'd at his achievement. But I spoke up, 'You could have gone by train or by plane with less effort. The company pays your expenses either way.' Then it occurred to me that I acted the same way about my shorthand—showing off my skill. The next morning I sold my boss on buying a dictating machine."

STATUS

Some girls oppose a dictating machine just to assert their own status. That's because their job imposes certain restrictions. They must be on time. They must do the work assigned to them, usually in a prescribed manner. But the boss can't tell them how to write shorthand! It's a skill that is individually possessed by the stenographer in her own little sphere. She alone can read its cryptic message. Her boss depends on her to transcribe it accurately. Maybe he can't recall what he dictated when she cannot decipher her notes. If she surrenders this skill to a machine, she feels that her sense of power is threatened.

This attitude of indispensability has its drawbacks. Suppose your boss has an unusual amount of work. If you stubbornly stick to stenography, he'll have to get another assistant. Or, suppose you are out sick. The girl who takes over may be more of a threat to your job than if your boss divides up some dictation among typists who are in the habit of reporting to you. In fact, it's a good idea to farm out work that is not too technical or confidential among typists, as a matter of course, so that they are prepared to step in if there is an emergency.

SKILL

"What about the bewildering machines, computing devices, and index systems found in many offices today? Should you bother with them, or attend strictly to pad, pencil and typewriter?" is a question brought up in an article, "You Are a Stenographer and You Want to Move Up," in *Charm* magazine.

The answer is:

The smart girl takes on as many machines as she reasonably can, leaving to the experts only the complex electronic ones that require full-time operation. There's never any telling when an unexpected skill will single you out for promotion.

Not long ago the traffic manager of a hardware firm needed a girl to assist his secretary with the Kardex system. Peggy was the only stenographer in the pool of twenty who knew how to handle this indexing method. She helped out for two weeks. A month later when his secretary left, the traffic manager requested Peggy for his secretary. The traffic manager is now a vice-president of the company, in line for the presidency, and Peggy is traveling right along with him.

The operation of most machines adds to our skill. The skills that are relinquished are inconsequential. The bookkeeper who prided herself that she could add a column of figures in her head is glad that she does not have to do so. Less and less do you notice advertisements asking for the application to be in handwriting. The "fine Spencerian hand" is no longer a marketable asset.

Shorthand is in a slightly different category. The machine is its servant—not a substitute. Many girls use both skills. An executive in a Houston oil company had used a dictating machine ever since the first crude models were available. But since his business took him increasingly into the field, from where he telephoned to the home office, his secretary used her shorthand to take down verbal instructions. Girls who take notes at meetings, do research in libraries, accompany their bosses on trips, use shorthand and dictating machines interchangeably.

Therefore, one of the questions in our survey was, "Will a dictating machine cause loss of technique?" We talked with a group of government stenographers in the Pentagon. "A machine can help improve shorthand," was their consensus. These girls were anxious to advance to higher ratings. They practiced shorthand from the transcriber whenever they had free time. Soon they found they could turn the machine to a faster speed—and take more words per minute—than when they passed their original tests.

Even without such practice, it normally takes only a week or two of concentrated effort to restore shorthand speed. You don't forget how to swim, or drive a car, just because you don't do it for a few years.

FATIGUE

As more and more women double as office workers and homemakers, the element of fatigue is gaining in importance. Electric typewriters get a high score as fatigue fighters. Babcock & Wilcox Company's New York headquarters uses every make of electric typewriter, according to a report in the Wall Street Journal. The office manager states he has found that girls using electric typewriters for correspondence make fewer errors in the late afternoon. Another finding was that girls who are shifted back from electrics to manuals "go home all worn out after a day's work."

Is stenography or operating a dictating machine more fatiguing? We interviewed two secretaries in a tool manufacturing company in Pasadena—girls who would be quick to notice signs of strain, since they were accustomed to work at a more or less leisurely tempo. Moreover, both were married and combined running a home with an office job.

The first girl smiled, "It's easier to plug in a vacuum cleaner than sweep with a broom, isn't it?" Her companion added, "It made me more tired waiting around half a day in the boss's office while he talked over the telephone . . . all the time knowing some of the mail had to be finished that day. Now I know what's ahead. It's less monotonous, too. You hear the material only once. Before, you wrote everything twice."

EFFICIENT USE OF MACHINES

Whether or not you were influential in the installation of an office machine, your instinctive womanly thrift will want to see it utilized to its best advantage. Otherwise, you may kill the chances for the installation of other labor saving devices.

Some points you can keep in mind are:

1. You will have to discover the rhythm or tempo of work with a machine that best suits your personality. An office machine is different from the "assembly line" because you set your own pace. Operating an office machine may be compared to playing a piano. You are its master.

2. A machine is no substitute for careful workmanship. Occasionally you will hear the remark, "We have machines, yes, but the work doesn't get out any faster than before." Here is what happened in one of these instances:

Nan was given an electric typewriter which considerably speeded her work. Because it went so fast, she took less pains to be accurate. "It takes me only a minute now to do it over," was her excuse for making mistakes. Those extra minutes consumed the time originally saved.

3. The economy of the electronic equipment is determined by how extensively it is used. Some girls possessively want a "one man machine." If another person borrows it, they whine, "Everytime she uses my machine, she changes the set-up. Now, if she wants it, I tell her I'm going to use it myself. That way I keep it for my own work."

Uneconomical utilization also results when girls oppose centralization of typing, accounting, or duplicating services. They "want to make an empire out of their desk," is how one office manager describes this attitude. "All work must be done in their immediate realm—even if they have to do it themselves—no matter how much others may be inconvenienced by the delay."

4. Inventing new uses for your machine makes you a work simplification expert. A cash register will give the number and amount of sales during a day. A cashier in a department store office wrote the time of the day on the paper roll once each hour. This segregated peak rush hours and enabled management to schedule the clerks for better service.

WHO'S PUSHING BUTTONS NOW?

Not too long ago, the importance of an executive was judged by the number of buttons he could command to summon assistants and secretaries.

Today, the girl in the office is pushing the buttons, or turning on the switches, that bring to her assistance modern office equipment devices. She can make the most of her job, if she is willing to make the most of the machines that are ready to serve her.

CHAPTER XI

We All Have Our Problems

DURING an average day, a group of six girls in a smoothly running office mentioned their problems to each other on eleven different occasions. Each time they lost anywhere from three minutes to a quarter of an hour. Problems ranged from perplexing to pressing. They were caused by the boss, the customers, fellow office employees and the company. In varying degrees, these problems had the girls emotionally disturbed. One couldn't eat any lunch, she was so upset. Another kept making typing mistakes. A third snapped at a customer over the telephone. Another kept biting her nails. Yet the experiences of these girls were not anything unique in business.

In fact, problems come up every day no matter how good relations are in an office. And we must solve them ourselves. Executives are too preoccupied with their own problems to be helpful in our affairs. They respect people who can "fight their own battles."

HOW DO YOU REACT TO PROBLEMS?

1. You may simply give up or say, "What's the use?" Resign yourself to see what will happen, and meantime brood and grumble.
2. You may try to blame someone else—usually the boss.
3. Or, you may attack the problem head-on.

Some creditable solution can be found for every problem—although it may not be what we originally desired—when we devote more time to the solution than to thinking about the difficulties. The problem solving technique requires that we use our intellect as well as our emotions. Definite steps that will help you meet your problems "head on" are:

UNDERSTAND THE REAL NATURE OF YOUR PROBLEMS

A secretary to a wealthy man writes to Mary Haworth, the columnist, that her problem is how to reject his Christmas gift. Her salary is paid by the company. Every year, her boss gives her a Christmas gift of $50—which is considerably less than she is drawing each week. He also gives $50 to his chauffeur, and several others in his employ. "I would much rather that he give me nothing, if he needs the money so badly that this is all he can spare," she writes. "Then I could keep my pride."

Miss Haworth answers:

"Actually, it isn't true that you don't want your employer's gift of $50. You're simply furious because he doesn't give you twice that much or more, as you virtually say in another breath."

Problems much more serious than this are caused for the same basic reason: a conflict between what we want and what we think we want. The first step to solving problems is to make certain we know what the problem really is.

TRY TO ANALYZE THE REASON BEHIND BEHAVIOR

Psychologists spend a lifetime studying the effect of the subconscious on our actions. It's not to be expected that we observe our bosses or associates with any possibility of fully understanding all their behavior. But a little common sense will go a long way toward recognizing "the thought behind the deed."

A controller in a company manufacturing calculating machines was extremely punctilious about having all statements ready way in advance of deadlines. In fact, he was reluctant to take a vacation, fearing something might go wrong.

On one occasion he had been unexpectedly invited to go fishing. "Everything is on schedule and I have more than enough work to keep me busy while you're gone," the girl in his office reassured him, as he was debating whether the press of duties would permit him to accept.

In spite of her statement, he stayed late for several nights to prepare some additional work for her. "Just in case you run short," he remarked as he handed the material to her.

The girl resented this insinuation that she did not have enough to do. How much did he think she could accomplish in a few short days, anyway? Didn't he trust her when she said she'd be kept busy? And so on.

She should have understood that the controller was compelled to complete the additional work to ease his own conscience. He had to provide for any possible emergency. He was not one to run off on pleasure trips wasting precious time! The hours he would spend on the trip had to be made up by working in advance.

Handing her the work was merely incidental and no reflection on her efficiency. He had no conception of how long it would take her to complete it, nor did he intend to imply that she did not have enough to do. He was motivated solely by the desire to justify his absence.

CONSIDER THE POSITION OF OTHERS INVOLVED

A public relations assistant in a Chamber of Commerce office found herself in a peculiar predicament. She had originally worked in the office of Mr. Sims, president of a hardware concern. When Mr. Sims was elected president of the Chamber, he suggested that this girl be added to the staff to handle the details of a "Beautify Your City" campaign which he wanted to promote during his term of office.

Technically, she was under the jurisdiction of the executive vice president of the Chamber—a permanent paid official whose position had tenure, whereas the presidency rotated from year to year.

Friction soon developed between the executive vice president and the girl. For example, she would write a publicity release. If she brought it first to him prior to getting the approval of Mr. Sims, the executive vice president would tell her to leave it with him—he would get the approval himself. Then he'd let the copy stay on his desk almost indefinitely—not intentionally, but because he was busy with an already full schedule. If she went directly to Mr. Sims for approval, the vice president was annoyed that she had by-passed him. If she did nothing, Mr. Sims wanted to know why the campaign was lagging.

In despair she talked to Mr. Sims and he promised to call a three-cornered meeting to see if he could straighten things out. That week-end, the girl tried to put herself in Mr. Sims' place. "He can't afford to antagonize the executive vice president," she reasoned. "The vice president, on the other hand, fears he will lose some prestige if I clear with Mr. Sims direct." She concluded that because of the position each man was in, the solution was up to her.

On Monday morning she telephoned Mr. Sims to call off the meeting. When she wrote her next piece of publicity, she attached a letter of transmittal, addressed to Mr. Sims, but to be signed by the executive vice president. Substantially, this letter read: "I have approved of the attached release. If you are in agreement, our office here at the Chamber will go ahead with this publicity."

Thus the executive vice president was not by-passed, since he signed the letter. A clear and prompt course of action was indicated which required no effort or decision on his part. The campaign was not delayed. Mr. Sims was kept informed. She had worked out a solution acceptable to all concerned.

GET THE FACTS

A library clerk in an investment concern was sullen. "I'm supposed to have a rest period between ten and ten-fifteen in the morning. If I leave the desk unattended, the people who come in are delayed till I return. If I wait for the librarian to relieve me, it sometimes takes till eleven o'clock, as she is often in conference. Why can't a girl from the research department replace me for this short period?"

This girl hasn't tried to find out whether the librarian purposely arranges the conferences at this hour, or whether she is called to such conferences without prior notice herself.

Nor does the girl know whether this rest period is general throughout the company, or whether she is specially privileged because she is in the library. Perhaps to have someone in from the research department would not be feasible if that department does not have prescribed rest periods.

Is the librarian strict about hours? Or does she graciously switch lunch hours if the clerk has an unexpected date? Has the clerk ever told the librarian that she feels strongly about having her rest period at a set time? And if so, why?

We are all too likely to jump to conclusions when we don't know the underlying facts.

CHECK TO SEE IF YOU ARE CONTRIBUTING TO THE PROBLEM

"I take dictation from several men, all of whom are of about equal rank," a young secretary stated. "Sometimes, when I'm with the methods engineer, the time study engineer telephones me. This time study man is extremely modest in his demands. Besides, he is usually out in the plant.

"Of course, I have to tell him that I'm busy with the methods engineer. He resents this. 'I come in so seldom, I should think I'd be able to get your services right away, especially as the methods engineer occupies so much of your time,' he protests.

"When I reported this back to the methods engineer, he answered, 'I don't care how little he is in the office. I don't like to be disturbed when I'm in the middle of a piece of work.'"

Since she is a woman, this girl ought to be smart enough to keep two men happy. But it makes her feel the center of attention to have two men bidding for her services. Unconsciously, she fans the flame, by telling each one what the other said.

She ought to ask the time study man to try to let her know in advance when he expects to be in. Then she can check ahead of time with the methods man on those days to see if he has any rush work so she can finish it before the other man arrives.

Discover Whether Your Problem Is Caused by One Individual or by the Group

An occasional difference with another individual should not disturb you. But if you feel yourself to be "different," or that others are ganging up on you, it's time to take stock.

Lydia tells us, [wrote Doris Blake, the columnist] that she happens to be a very quiet girl, whereas the girls in her office are just the opposite. Because of this, Lydia feels out of place.
"There are many times I can go days without having conversation with any of them. Now, it seems they talk about me and are very annoyed that I do not mix with them. Lately they do not seem to bother with or about me and that makes me feel bad and uncomfortable here. I like my job and while I feel like quitting sometimes, I do not want to do it. The girls just do not seem to

care for me and I do not understand why. I hope you can give me some advice."

Miss Blake answered:

Well, young lady, if you were up on your job qualifications, you'd realize that getting along with co-workers is deemed one of the great essentials. That old-time drudge plan of working to the exclusion of every phase of compatibility with your co-workers is not one of our modern day occupational blessings.

Personality traits in employees, whether for good or ill, have come to mean more in business organizations, and this applies more to women than to men. There is nothing very healthy in working in an atmosphere in which one feels like an outsider. It is not a cooperative spirit. And in your case, Lydia, you are obviously to blame for the ostracism you are now suffering.

You brought it on yourself by your own lack of friendliness. You can be quiet and still be a friendly person. We think perhaps you have diagnosed your quietness wrong. There's no doubt that your co-workers feel that way, too. You have in all probability given the impression that you are a bit high-hat, superior as it were, revealed in your hint that the other girls are not as quiet and refined as you.

Discover Whether the Person Who Causes Your Problems Acts the Same to Everyone Else

Lydia brought on her problems herself. *Glamour* magazine printed a problem which illustrates a converse situation.

In a new job, I met a co-worker who had been with the company for many years, and who made things very unpleasant for me by her arrogance and open antagonism. She assigned me a very early lunch hour, didn't introduce me to anyone, whispered and giggled with the others behind my back. I had to decide whether to give up a job I liked or to ride out an unpleasant situation after examining the whys and wherefores.

Here is how this woman solved her problem:

I liked the job, so decided to ride out the unpleasantness. Eventually, I was glad I did so, because I found out, after I had been there several months, that this was her usual behavior. She was unpleasant to everyone and resented anyone new who showed initiative or who could take responsibility. She was finally asked to leave because of her attitude. The incident taught me to have patience, not to be so self-deprecatory, that I would believe myself always at fault and to realize that it was possible for me to be right and the other person to be wrong. Too often a sense of insecurity will make you put the blame on yourself and as a result you will make hurried, ill-considered moves. My job has turned out wonderfully well and I am glad I learned to look beyond myself.

GIVE OTHERS THE BENEFIT OF THE DOUBT

A junior cost accountant in a company manufacturing boilers spent all morning on some comparative figures showing the difference between the cost of power as produced by the company's own facilities and the power purchased from the local utility. Her boss, a vice president, wanted these figures for a 1:30 P. M. meeting, so she had only a cup of coffee and sandwich sent in, and worked through her lunch hour to finish the estimate.

Meanwhile, the vice president went out for lunch with some members of the board of directors. When he returned, she brought him the completed report, proud it was so promptly done. "Thanks," he took it absentmindedly, and put the estimates in his desk drawer. She found he had left them there when he departed for the meeting at 1:30.

"To think," she confided to a friend, "he didn't need them this afternoon at all! I could have had all day to do the job!" She feels her boss is such a problem!

What had actually happened? The vice president was convinced that it was cheaper for the company to manufacture its own power. He wanted figures to prove his point. The estimate prepared by the junior accountant showed him to be right, too.

Then at the luncheon one of the directors announced that the local utility had just given the company an order for several large boilers. Obviously, this was not an auspicious moment to curtail buying power from the utility! The vice president mentally shelved his proposal. And naturally, the report which the junior cost accountant had prepared would serve no purpose at the meeting in view of what had transpired.

Of course, the vice president could have told her about these circumstances. But he was too disappointed himself that his cost-saving proposal on this occasion was side-tracked. If the girl had given him the benefit of the doubt, she would not have felt he was a "problem." She would have assumed that he must have had a reason to justify his request for the estimates.

Realize That Others Have the Same Problems

It helps to know that no matter how different you think your problem is, others have similar problems.

"Many a girl has chewed her fingernails to the quick hunting desperately for that letter the boss wants immediately," says an article in *Transcription Supervisors' Association Echo*. "It turns up precisely at 4:38 on his desk in the current folder. Mr. Doakes dictates the reply to be typed that same night. Alternating a mutter with a prayer, she bats out the finished product by 4:55 and rushes the precious document to him—only to be greeted with, 'Oh, I want to send an enclosure along. Tomorrow will do!'"

At Lederle Laboratories, in Pearl River, New York, girls had this to say about "That Man in the Office:"

"Why does he insult me by keeping his desk locked when he's away?"

"Why must he wave wildly like a mad maestro to get my attention, instead of using my name?"

"My boss goes to training classes to learn how to cope with this situation and that situation—but when the situation arises, how does he cope with it? The same old way."

"Bosses aren't a bad lot. Treat them right and they'll reciprocate."

Bosses, too, had their say:

"She acts like a mother to me—always protecting me!"

"I don't like her to sign my name to everything."

"She seems to be eating all day."

"I don't like the way girls talk, in such places as the ladies room, about their bosses and about their work—things which should be part of a confidential relationship."

"With all her faults, she's wonderful, anyway."

FIND OUT HOW YOUR PROBLEM IS HANDLED ELSEWHERE

Sometimes we fail to get the proper perspective on our problems. Exploring how other offices operate, getting an objective view, "throwing some light on the matter," won't hurt.

Carolyn was discontented because her boss did not like her to have so many personal telephone calls. She was discussing her grievance with a girl friend who said, "My boss doesn't object to calls. I get a couple of calls almost every week."

Carolyn was suddenly silent. She had three or four calls a day! She quickly perceived that her boss was justified in his attitude.

TAKE CONSTRUCTIVE ACTION

"The financial editor always asks me to borrow books or magazines from other editors," a secretary says peevishly. "Then he keeps them for weeks. The people from whom I've borrowed them seem to think it's my fault if I don't bring them back. I don't have the stuff!"

She makes no attempt to be constructive. For instance:

1. She could check with the editor to see whether he's through with certain publications from time to time, and return them to their owners. Doubtless he just pushes them aside, and covers them with more recent material, or keeps them in his brief case.

2. She can ask him what material he needs from the books and make excerpts. These might be even handier for him, since they can be made in duplicate, and appropriately filed. This would enable her to return the books in question almost immediately.

3. She might check the library to see if the same books are available and secure them from that source, rather than borrowing personal copies from individuals.

4. If the office has suitable equipment, she can have the material photostated.

5. She can telephone the people from whom the books have been borrowed to let them know the boss still has them in his office and she is "keeping her eye" on them and will return them as soon as possible.

Her indifference sometimes irritates the people in the office as much as the inconvenience caused by not getting their material back promptly.

MAKE DECISIONS PROMPTLY

Most of us have difficulty making decisions. Maybe we can't make up our mind because we wonder whether what we think should be done is right. Or perhaps we fear the criticism of others.

Delay in making decisions affects our own peace of mind and causes problems for others. And if we subsequently don't stick to our decisions, our troubles mount. We have all witnessed the havoc caused by the indecisive automobile driver who waits at a crossing and then starts out just as the other driver finally moves ahead. The following case illustrates the problem that can result from vacillating action:

Alice was put in charge of a new comptometry division. "You'll need an assistant—someone who can take over when you are out. How about Lucille from the payroll department?" the office manager suggested.

After a week's trial, Alice definitely decided Lucille wouldn't do and sent her back to payroll. Then Alice interviewed half a dozen applicants from outside the organization but did not test any of them. All the while she was worried about what the others would say when they found she wasn't taking a girl from within the company. Maybe she should give Lucille another chance after all.

When Lucille was once more promoted, she boasted to her friends, "Guess Alice couldn't find anyone as good as me!" She acted as if she were indispensable. Her work, only fair before, was even less acceptable. But Alice didn't dare change her mind again!

BE PROUD OF YOUR DECISION

Both James Christie, department head of a Wall Street law firm, and one of his assistants, Vincent Leonard, did outside legal work. Christie always paid the department secretary, Betty, for copying his briefs, asking her to do the work on her own time. Leonard, on the other hand, implied he would like her to "work in" his typing when she had free time. Then, a day or two later, he'd check up whether it was done. In order to finish it as fast as possible, she sometimes sacrificed her office duties to accommodate him.

Betty didn't like her office work to slide, but she didn't want to stay on her own time to do Leonard's work without compensation. She finally decided to tell Mr. Christie about Leonard's surreptitious tactics.

Betty did not solve her problem by her action. She felt guilty that she had complained about Leonard behind his back. Mr. Christie was piqued that right along he had been paying for personal work while his assistant had been getting free service. He offered to speak to Leonard, insisting that Betty be paid, but she didn't want that. Leonard would learn that she had discussed the matter with the boss and would be annoyed. The entire incident left a "bad taste."

How much better would it have been if Betty had told Leonard herself that she could not do his work on office time, that others paid her for private jobs, and that if he wanted his work done on company time, he'd have to clear directly with Mr. Christie. She could then have been proud of her straightforward approach to a delicate situation.

BE WILLING TO COMPROMISE

Sometimes we're convinced we have the answer to a problem. Then we try to force acceptance of our solution on others, rather than working toward a mutually acceptable compromise.

A girl in a real estate office insisted that she could never get out her work on time because her boss only dictated one letter whenever he called her in. "That means wasting ten minutes to half an hour doing nothing, after I finish, till he calls me in again," was the way she put her problem. She informed her boss, "The only way I'll be able to finish each day is if you give me the correspondence in a well-organized batch."

The real estate dealer's contention was he always had to consult his listings, make telephone calls, estimate costs, before he was ready to dictate on each of the respective communications. He wouldn't be able to start on his letters till after lunch if he wanted to do it in a batch, because it would take him all morning to get his information. Besides, it was easier to get one project off his mind before concentrating on a new one.

In this case, the girl was shown that there were alternatives to dictating the mail in a batch. She and her boss worked out a master letter, much of which she could type as soon as the inquiries were received. Space was left for the listings and special information which could be filled in later when available.

FACE THE FACT THAT SOME PROBLEMS HAVE NO PERFECT SOLUTION

Some problems can be solved in several ways.

Ingrid worked for both Mr. Edler, treasurer of an electrical manufacturer, and for his assistant, Mr. Penner. When Mr. Penner was promoted to the vice presidency, he asked Ingrid to come along with him.

Ingrid liked both men, but decided to stay with Mr. Edler. Not long after, through a shift in executive ranks, Mr. Edler unexpectedly resigned. This left her high and dry. Mr. Penner had in the meantime hired a girl from the outside who was proving satisfactory.

Luckily, this case had a happy ending. Six months later, Mr. Edler, bored with retirement, became a consultant. Remembering Ingrid's loyalty, he invited her to work with him again.

SUMMARY

We all have plenty of problems. The pattern of our problems tends to repeat itself, too, because our individual personalities tend to create the same type of situation. Review your past problems and you will have a preview of what to expect.

Even when you reach a permanent solution of one problem, you may be faced with another version of the same sort in the near future.

No one has ever found a set formula for arriving at solutions. If we do something, and it turns out wrong, we feel we should have waited. If we do nothing—which also involves a decision—and our problem is not solved, we feel we should have acted. Even the ancient proverbs contradict themselves: "Look before you leap," and "He who hesitates is lost."

CHAPTER XII

Make the Most of Maturity

IN SOME careers, a woman reaches a definite point when she considers herself mature. A teacher sees the children of her former pupils coming to school. An actress is given a "mother" role. Models have petitioned that they be permitted to deduct "depreciation" because their careers are so short-lived.

The business woman faces no such crucial period. We are not conscious of her as belonging to any age group. She may not stay young, but she does not grow old. We associate her with her accomplishments, her reputation for efficiency, her status in the company.

ASSETS OF MATURITY

Maturity actually gives a business woman a number of assets—both to herself and the organization she works for.

FINANCIAL SUCCESS

From the standpoint of achieving success, these are the best years of her life. The highest salaries are paid to mature women. In the federal service, more than half of the women in the upper-salaried jobs were over forty-five when they reached top brackets. The National Secretaries Association recently selected a thirty-eight-year-old woman as "secretary of the year." The woman who has been with the company a number of years is usually considered indispensable to her boss and paid accordingly.

STABILITY

Older women show their stability by being more prompt, less likely to be absent, more conscientious, more serious about their jobs. Executives feel it is in their favor that they do not have their minds on "dates."

The mature woman has learned to handle men, either through her marriage or through her business experience.

Mrs. Todd, in her late thirties, and Sally, a recent high school graduate, had just left the office of the head cashier. "I'm ready to quit," Sally was almost crying. "I did all those reports just as he told me—and then he says I'm wrong. He's impossible!"

"Sally," Mrs. Todd calmed her down, "you heard he was also accusing me of not following his instructions. Life is that way. My husband often blames me for things that go wrong around the house whether it's my fault or not. But I certainly wouldn't walk out on him!"

SKILL AND EXPERIENCE

Obviously, the longer a person is in business, the more she acquires skill in her specific work. She is also capable of doing a greater variety of jobs.

The older woman continues to improve her skills, too. In jobs that require dexterity as well as skill and thought she may decrease in speed of movement (generally only after she is sixty) but there is a continuous improvement in precision and judgment.

Dr. Edward J. Stieglitz points out in a pamphlet of the Women's Bureau of the United States Department of Labor that "throughout maturity people can learn nearly as rapidly as teen-agers. Many older women learn more selectively, more accurately, and with better grasp of relationships."

PRESTIGE

The confidence and composure inspired by the mature receptionists and secretaries in offices of doctors, dentists, psychiatrists and hospitals is a recognized asset. In the business office, older women often suggest conservatism.

An executive remarked, "When I called on the J-N Company, I was impressed by all the older, serious women in the office. They must be a sound, well-established organization."

On the other hand, a teen-age secretary may detract from a man's prestige. A department head confided to an associate, "Our new president evidently isn't going to do much work himself. I guess he'll pass most of his responsibilities on to the executive vice president."

"What makes you think so?" the associate asked.

"Didn't you see the beautiful young secretary he hired? If he were going to run things personally, he'd need an older, more experienced woman."

YOUR BEST BEHAVIOR

Maturity has its advantages. Few women, however, want to be accepted merely on the basis of the assets which have naturally accrued during the years of work. They want to make sure, at the same time, that they do not fall into patterns of behavior which distinguish them disadvantageously from younger groups.

Suggestions passed on to us by executives include:

1. Study youthful habits. Women spend too much time talking about their physical condition. "I can't stand on my feet all day any more," a bank teller sighs. Actually, she never had been able to stand on her feet for long periods. As a teen-ager, she fainted while waiting for a seat in the movies. Everyone gets tired sometimes—why emphasize that as a sign of age?

"Remember, we're not so young as we used to be," a woman who has made up the payrolls for a number of years tells her co-workers at the slightest provocation. Nobody is! But Dr. Lydia G. Giberson, of the Metropolitan Life Insurance Company, has found that the woman who is mature and in good health "has great reserves of endurance and recovers rapidly from fatigue."

The older woman often is seeking reassurance when she draws attention to her age. She wants to be contradicted. "You don't look a day older than when you first came," is what she hopes to hear. Instead, she makes people aware of her real or imagined deficiencies by angling for compliments.

Men are more influenced by behavior than actual age.

An attorney was appointed director of a government office. He informed the Civil Service agency that he would like to have Mrs. Watson, the administrative assistant who currently held the job, transferred. "Confidentially," he added, "she's too old, too slow in getting around." Mrs. Watson was thirty-nine. The woman he promoted to be her successor was forty-two. When this inconsistency was pointed out to him, he defended his choice. "There's a world of difference. Mrs. Watson gives the appearance of being middle-aged and matronly. The new woman is dignified, snappy and full of pep."

2. Develop self-confidence. Self-confidence is more important to older women than to younger ones, says Albert Edward Wiggam, the psychologist. "Younger people feel they have plenty of time to cure defects and drawbacks. Not so with women over forty. Psychologists in many firms are trying to show older people that their supposed handicaps are not due to age, but to worrying about age."

3. Be flexible about fashion. A writer once said, "When I think of my mother, I always remember her as being about thirty-five." Many older women, likewise, seem to cling to the

idea that they look as they did when they first came to work. They stick to fashions they liked when they were younger. Yet fashion magazines and newspapers are full of advice on how to make the most of yourself from a fashion and beauty angle at different periods of your life.

Women who aren't fashionable become a problem to their boss. He may appreciate their good work. But he doesn't like it if other executives ridicule his department as being "full of fuddy-duddies." He may have worked with these women over a period of years. Instinctively he feels he is in the same age group as they are and this makes him seem older himself.

4. Keep up with the boss mentally. Modern literature has dealt with the self-made man whose wife has not kept up with him mentally. The woman in business who does not keep up with her boss—especially if he is the type who is "going places" will find herself in the same predicament.

Mr. Braden started with the company as an engineer, when Selma—just out of high school—was assigned to him. Braden took his Master's degree evenings. He was selected to attend a management development course, and in time became vice president for engineering and design.

Periodically, he mentioned to Selma that it would be helpful if she would take some courses, but she shrugged off his suggestions. "I'm rushed enough already with the work I have," was her justification for indifference about further education.

After much deliberation, Mr. Braden eventually relegated Selma to a supervisory job in a typing pool. Braden liked Selma personally. They had worked together more than fifteen years. He arranged the transfer so that it seemed like a promotion. But in reality, the move was necessitated by the fact that Selma just had not kept pace with his growing requirements.

5. Be realistic about newcomers. Women who have worked faithfully for a number of years resent the fact that young

girls, starting in today, receive a salary which may be twice as much as they got when they started working.

The long-service employee also regards the newcomer as a potential threat to her job.

The situation is not improved if the older woman tries to put obstacles in the way of the new girl, withholds information, or excludes her from office social events. Executives are alert to such antagonistic attitudes. On the other hand, the older woman who is helpful to newcomers, stamps herself as a person with executive potentialities. As a consequence, she may even be offered a better position.

Inequities occur in every profession. The sales clerk in the store, the nurse, the telephone operator and many others reach maximum rates. After they are at the top of the bracket, there is no added pay advantage for further years of service. Even though the differential between your present salary and that of the girl just out of business school may not be too great, at least there are no arbitrary limitations to your future earnings in the majority of office jobs.

CHANGING JOBS

If you look around you in your office, or among your acquaintances, you'll agree that the mature woman who is established in her job is generally getting an excellent salary and has a position of prestige and authority. Even though she may have let herself slide, she is firmly entrenched and not likely to lose her job.

If, however, as a mature woman you are trying to re-enter the business world, or must change jobs, you face a problem. Despite the shortage of office workers, the historical prejudice against hiring older women still endures to a certain extent.

Altrusa International Clubs, a woman's service organization, made a survey of employers' attitudes in regard to hiring older women. Many felt that women past middle age are stuck in a rut, resist new ideas, are intolerant, lack initiative, are over-emotional, and talk too much. They are not so much against old age as against "old habits."

How and Where to Look for a Job

In looking for a job, we must counteract both the cold statistics of our chronological age, and the criticisms which executives make of the older woman's behavior. Here are some suggestions for a job-hunting campaign based on these considerations:

1. When you register at an employment agency, select one that caters to you. One agency directs its advertisements in *The New York Times* to "Mature Women Only," and states it has a department for "those who have been turned down because of age."

Try to listen in when the interviewer at the agency makes an appointment with a prospective employer. Interviewers have developed techniques of "selling" the mature woman which you can also follow in the contacts you create for yourself. For, besides using an agency, it is wise to supplement your efforts in other directions.

2. Your résumés should be "tailor made" to emphasize your qualifications as they apply to each specific job you investigate.

A. Group together your various experiences and interests in organizations similar to the one where you are seeking a job. A woman answering an advertisement for a job in a travel agency wrote:

For a five-year period, from 1933 to 1938, I was in charge of the Radio City office of the World Travel Bureau.

For three years, from 1939 to 1942, I was secretary to the Vice President of the Green Star Line.

In my present position as administrative assistant to an executive, I plan his itineraries, and arrange extensive trips for members of his family.

B. Highlight the duties you are capable of performing.

How can you prepare a résumé, [Mrs. K. E. wrote to "Opportunities Unlimited," a newspaper column] when your whole experience has been in volunteer work?

In my own particular volunteer job, I worked from 9 until 5, five days a week for 12 years.

I ran the office, did the personnel interviewing, ordered the supplies, saw that the mailing got out accurately and on time, and did all the other kinds of work involved in running an office. But the minute they see 12 years' volunteer work, they act as if all I had been doing was eating chocolates and reading magazines!

The columnist advised:

If the job is broken down into actual duties involved, it is easier for the employer to see that the person might fit into his job which involves similar duties.

For example, if you are making out a résumé for an office manager's job, you should not simply put down: "Experience— 12 years at such and such Society."

Instead, you would say:

Qualifications:

1. Ability to supervise a mass of detailed correspondence and paper work. (Go into this in detail giving the size of the mailings, number of typists, etc.)
2. Ability to screen and hire effective people with a minimum of turnover.
3. Ability to handle inquiries from the public, and give information accurately and rapidly.

By breaking the duties down in this way, it will be easier for the employer to see you as a potential office manager, than if you simply lumped your experience under 12 years in a volunteer job.

3. Use discretion in listing your previous jobs. Select only the positions, education and experience that are pertinent. (Of course, you must not leave any noticeable gaps. But you may have had one or two short duration jobs which need not be included because they break the continuity of your record. Also, some of your studies may not be particularly applicable.)

If your résumé lists too many former employers—no matter how good a reference they may give you—that creates the impression of instability.

4. Write unsolicited letters of application. In such letters you need not go out of your way to divulge your age. On the other hand, don't give the erroneous impression that you are a youngster. This might react to your disadvantage when you are asked to call.

5. Don't let aptitude tests confuse you. Fill them out as well as you can. Older women sometimes make the mistake of trying to hide some of their knowledge, fearing they will be considered over-qualified. Such an attempt is easily detected. It may boomerang later if a better job than the one you are applying for opens up.

6. Make your availability known to former associates—schoolmates, people with whom you have worked, and friends. They think of you as you were when you first met them, and are not so sensitive to your growing older.

7. Volunteer to do typing and clerical tasks for organizations like the Red Cross, Boy Scouts, parent-teacher Associations, veterans, ambulance corps, Women's Voters League, churches, alumnae, political parties. This may place you in direct contact with executives who are looking for someone. Or their wives may mention your skill to their husbands. It also keeps you in practice while you are waiting for something to develop.

8. Take a refresher course at a business school—whether you need it or not. Wear good clothes while attending school instead of saving them for job interviews. Many business concerns contact schools or even have representatives call in person for recruits. It pays to look your best all the time.

9. Canvass your immediate neighborhood. Your long residence in the same locality may have resulted in contacts that may be valuable to an employer. You will find good opportunities in real estate offices, where you might combine office

work with some selling. Administrative offices of smaller colleges, medical, philanthropic or welfare organizations are worth investigating. Personnel offices of factories sometimes prefer older women when the job involves paying off large groups of laborers.

Another reason why suburban areas are good hunting grounds is that the younger girls want to go to the cities where they hope for glamour jobs. With the rapid decentralization of business, the supply of office workers in smaller communities is limited, making older women more acceptable and welcome.

10. Don't discriminate against working for a woman. Young girls turn down women bosses because they prefer a man. The woman executive often likes an older woman. She is not prejudiced against age, since she is usually an older woman herself. And she may consider that a young, attractive girl in the same office with her offers an unfavorable comparison.

11. Show your willingness to adapt yourself to a job of lesser importance. Personnel directors state that they hesitate to offer positions with junior ratings to older women—especially women who have earned more. They feel such a woman will shortly become dissatisfied. Be forward looking during your interview. Don't dwell on past glories or "what used to be."

12. If you have been away from work for any length of time, convince your prospective employer that you can make the transition from home to office.

One woman raised doubts when she engaged the man who was interviewing her in a conversation about children. She noticed pictures of his children on his desk, and thought she could establish a point of contact with him by showing snapshots of her own youngsters.

Unfortunately, the pictures she showed had been taken a few years back. The employer decided that such a devoted mother, with children so young, would be too much worried about them to give full attention to her work.

Guard against intimating that you will "mother" the girls in the office. A personnel manager in a large aircraft company said, "No matter how desperately we need people, I will not place an older woman in a department with a number of young girls. She'll try to run their lives. They resent the interference and trouble starts."

It's also good policy to refrain from treating your prospective boss as you treat your husband's friends, even though you may be socially acquainted. Call him "Mr."

13. Don't let your brains show too much. A woman was offered a job as a typist. During the interview, the man who was hiring her mentioned that he was taking a course in a nearby college. She was on the verge of divulging that she had taken this course herself, and could help him with the homework. She wisely kept still.

Executives develop fear and resentment of mature women of accomplishment. Psychologists attribute this to feelings of inferiority on the part of men—particularly when they have risen to success without too much formal education.

14. Discount the impression of gray hair. The practice of touching up one's hair "for business reasons" has become widely accepted, particularly at the time when one is looking for a job, but it is no necessity.

Arlene, in her mid-forties, had considerable difficulty making the right connection. She felt her gray hair was the cause. A beautician convinced her she should have a rinse. The very next day Arlene landed a responsible position.

The personnel director, a woman, was perfectly aware that Arlene's hair was touched up. The reason Arlene was offered the job was not because she looked younger than she was, but because of her poise and self-assurance. In previous interviews, she had been self-conscious about her hair.

On the other hand, some girls with touched up hair are ill at ease when job seeking, for fear the deception will be detected.

So, whatever you decide about your hair, be sure that the minute you put on your hat and set out for your job interview, you can forget about how it looks.

15. Select a job which provides the best long-term security. The mature woman frequently makes a special effort to get a job with a company that has a pension plan. She would like to feel that she has something to fall back on when she retires. Meanwhile, companies with pension plans have difficulty fitting in people who come at a relatively late period in their careers, so her chances are correspondingly slimmer.

Keep in mind that in many cases, if you don't work for a company for a long period, your pension is rather a trifling amount. Because a pension plan is in effect, retirement is compulsory at a specified age. As a consequence, you will be faced with looking for some supplementary source of income at the time you retire.

From a practical standpoint, it is better to take a job, perhaps for slightly less pay, where your period of employment is not so specifically limited.

SUMMARY

Maturity is a state of mind. Like youth, it has both advantages and disadvantages. But in an office job its disadvantages can be turned into assets. The ideas set forth in this chapter should help you feel that as far as your career is concerned, "the best is yet to be, the last of life for which the first was made."

Index

DATE DUE

GAYLORD			PRINTED IN U.S.A.